Get More Referrals Now!

Get More Referrals Now!

Bill Cates

McGraw-Hill
New York Chicago San Francisco Lisbon London
Madrid Mexico City Milan New Delhi
San Juan Seoul Singapore Sydney Toronto

The McGraw-Hill Companies

1 2 3 4 5 6 7 8 9 0 DOC/DOC 0 9 8 7 6 5 4

ISBN 0-07-141775-3

McGraw-Hill books are available at special quantity discounts to use as premiums and sales promotions, or for use in corporate training programs. For more information, please write to the Director of Special Sales, McGraw-Hill Professional, Two Penn Plaza, New York, NY 10121-2298. Or contact your local bookstore.

This book is printed on recycled, acid-free paper containing a minimum of 50% recycled, de-inked fiber.

Library of Congress Cataloging-in-Publication Data

Cates, W. R. (William R.)
Get more referrals now! / by Bill Cates.
p. cm.
ISBN 0-07-141775-3 (alk. paper)
1. Business referrals. I. Title.
HF5438.25.C367 2003
658.8—dc22
2003025379

To my daughter, Jenna. She has taught me how to be open to many new possibilities. She has taught me about courage. She has taught me about love.

Contents

Acknowledgments

It's impossible to acknowledge all the people who have given me help and inspiration during the development of this project. Here are a few that stand out in my mind: Jenna Catherine Cates, Linda Cates, Lee Bristol, Kris Cates-Bristol, Jessica Cates-Bristol, John Hurley, Randy Richie, Jay Magenheim, Joel Rosenberg, Les Picker, Terrie Lupberger, David Lupberger, Phil Simonides, Willie Jolley, Jim Ball, Steven Gaffney, Ron Culberson, Wolf Rinke, Karen Hood, Ron Lanio, Bruce Bordelon, Ray Vendetti, and Barry Neville (my editor at McGraw-Hill).

Introduction

THE MOST IMPORTANT SALE I EVER MADE

Can you remember the first thing you ever sold? Go way back into your youth. Was it lemonade? Candy? Cookies? Greeting cards? I remember my first sales experience as if it were yesterday.

I was 9 years old. I was a Cub Scout in Kensington, Maryland—Pack 456, Den 2. Our pack needed to raise money, so someone decided we'd hold a sales contest. The product? Furnace filters. The prize? A brand new, royal blue, 26-inch, three-speed Schwinn bicycle. Man, did I want to win that Schwinn. I'd be the first kid on my block to own a three-speed.

I knew I was going to win that bike. I owned that bike in my mind before the first shipment of furnace filters arrived. I went downstairs to the laundry room and took a few clothespins from my mom's hamper. Then I slipped out a few playing cards from a deck in my father's dresser. What was I going to do with these cards? You know! I'd put four on the front spokes and four on the back spokes. My motor!

On July 16, 1960—the hottest day of the year—the furnace filters arrived. Who in their right mind would try to sell furnace filters in the dead of summer?

There I stood with furnace filter samples and order forms in hand. My mother pushed me out of the door like a mother bird pushes her baby out of the nest for its first flight. Cold calling door to door! You know, your neighborhood is usually a pretty friendly place when you're a kid—until you try to *sell* something. Doors were slammed in my face. People who I could see were at home ignored me. The fiberglass filters itched my sweaty skin—but I wanted that Schwinn.

After going up one side of my street and down the other—no sales yet—I faced my biggest fear: knocking on the door where the Wilks family lived. Dimmie and Bill Wilks, with their daughters, Adrienne and Sharon, were friends of our family, but to me, Mr. Wilks was the ogre of the neighborhood.

Almost every day during the summer, and many days during the school year, neighborhood kids gathered in the dead end to play baseball. Third base was on Mr. Wilks front lawn, and he didn't care for that. Almost every day this scene played itself out. We'd be playing ball in the dead end. Around 5:30 p.m., Mr. Wilks would come home from work in his yellow Ford Galaxy 500. He'd flash his lights and lay on his horn to chase us away. His jumping out of his car would signal the end of our game for that day. The neighborhood kids would scatter.

There I stood at Mr. Wilks's front door, hoping and praying that Mrs. Wilks would answer. When Mr. Bill Wilks opened the door, I was shaking in my shoes.

"Hey, Billy Cates," he said. "What ya got there?"

I gave him my best (my only) sales pitch: "I'm selling furnace filters for the Cub Scouts. You don't want any do you?"

"Well, I might take a couple if you have the right size. Come on in while I check what size I need for my furnace."

Wow! The ogre of the neighborhood was being nice to me. I sat down on his sofa while he went into the basement to check his furnace. I had the right size. He ordered two. My first sale! I was excited.

It turned out that Mr. Wilks was a salesman—a very successful salesman. He asked me a question I will never forget. "So, Billy

Cates. Going door to door, eh? Cold calling? Not an easy thing. Tell me, son, what's your closing ratio?"

"Huh?"

"How many houses have you been to and how many sales have you made?"

"Oh, well, let's see. I've been to 10 houses ... and you're my first sale."

"Well, that's 10 percent. Not bad for *cold calling*. Would you like to do better?"

Of course I did. I was about to get my first sales training at the age of 9 as a Cub Scout selling furnace filters door to door.

He told me, "When we're done here, go across the dead end to the D'Angelos. You know them. When Mr. or Mrs. D'Angelo answers the door, say that I sent you there, that I just bought two filters, and ask them how many they want. It's that simple. When you're done with them, find out who their neighbor is and keep repeating the process. Got that?"

Off I went. I was even more excited than before because now I had a strategy. Well, Mr. Wilks was right. Mrs. D'Angelo bought two filters from me and sent me to her neighbors. The Jacobsons bought two. The Kleins bought two. So did the Termans, Murphys, and Yees. I sold more filters that summer than almost the entire pack of 38 boys—and you guessed it—I won that Schwinn!

Why did I win that contest? Three simple, but powerful, lessons came from that experience: First, I had a burning desire. My desire for success kept me going in the face of poor initial results and even fear. Second, I had a powerful strategy. I learned the effectiveness of referrals. And third, I learned the importance of courage. Without the courage to apply Mr. Wilks's lesson, I would certainly not have won that bike.

Mr. Wilks became my mentor in sales. I even worked for him as a sales assistant later in high school and college. He taught me another powerful lesson.

"Billy, you know one thing that all successful people have in common?" he asked one day.

"No," I replied.

"They have long necks. That's right. All successful people have long necks. They're willing to 'stick their necks out' and take the risks necessary to get better all the time. Keep sticking your neck out, Billy. Don't be afraid to make mistakes. Don't be afraid to fail. There's no disgrace in failure. There's only disgrace in not trying."

Thank you for this lesson, Mr. Wilks!

THE WAY OF THE WORLD

If you accept that the world of business revolves around meeting people, you'll understand one of my company's slogans, "The way of the world is meeting people through other people, and the referral is the warm way we get into people's lives." When you need to find a painter to paint your home, do you go to the phone book first? No, you ask friends and neighbors for recommendations. When you need to find a babysitter for your child, do you stop the kids walking by your house on the way home from school? No, you ask neighbors. Your best clients want to meet you through an introduction from someone they already trust. That's why the referral process should be your primary method for attracting new clients.

I've been using the principles, strategies, and skills in this book for years, and they've helped me build several successful businesses. I've been sharing them through my presentations to salespeople, sales managers, and business owners for over 12 years. Now I've put all the information together in a systematic approach. This book is the blueprint you will need to build a successful referral-based business.

THE MOST POWERFUL WAY TO ATTRACT NEW CLIENTS

Without question, attracting clients through referrals is the most powerful way to build your business, not to mention the most enjoy-

able. Chris Faicco, an executive with Northwestern Mutual Life, conducted one of many studies that clearly quantifies the power of referrals. Of 5,640 qualified suspects, 2,240 were turned into prospects by cold calls, and the remaining 3,400 were converted into prospects by referrals. The cold call prospects yielded 56 sales, or an 11 percent closing ratio. The referral prospects yielded 452 sales, or a 40 percent closing ratio. In other words, the chances of making the sale *were almost four times greater with referrals.*

If you don't sell life insurance, you may be thinking, "What does this have to do with me?" Everything. Sure, the ratios in your industry may be a little different, but you wouldn't be reading this book if you didn't already have a clear sense that building your business from referrals is the best route to success.

When you prospect for new clients over the telephone via cold calls, you usually get the cold shoulder. The prospects say things like, "Send information," "I'm already covered in that area," or "We're happy with our current supplier." When you market through direct mail, you spend a great deal of time and money for a very small percentage of results. When you market through advertising, you spend a great deal of money and never quite know what the results are. When you market through seminars, your cost-per-lead can be extremely high.

With the emergence of the do-not-call regulations, not only is cold calling becoming less effective, it can cost you dearly in penalties if you call the wrong person. (See Chapter 1.) With a referral-based business, you're attracting people the way they want to meet you—through a trusted friend or business associate.

ETHICAL OPPORTUNISM

Why don't all businesspeople build their businesses from referrals? Quite frankly, this baffles me. Certainly, when you are first starting out in business, you might have to prospect in other ways to get the ball rolling and create a critical mass of activity. Certainly, some businesses lend themselves to referral marketing more than others, but I've never run into a salesperson or business owner who can't use the methods I teach in this book to increase his or her client base, sales, and profitability.

I think part of the problem is that, until recently, there has been very little teaching in this area. Even Tom Hopkins's classic sales book, *How to Master the Art of Selling* (Tom Hopkins International, 1982), calls the referral the "backbone of prospecting for champions," yet he spends only a page and a half on referral marketing.

If you go to a book store or library and look for a book on referrals, you're more likely to end up with a book on "networking." While networking is an important component in referral marketing (see Part Three of this book), it's only a part of the referral creation process.

I think it's time to elevate referral marketing to a new level of professionalism. Marketing expert Jay Abraham uses the phrase "ethical opportunism." Other people call it leverage. As you serve people better and create relationships of trust, a little proactivity on your part will yield many opportunities for all parties—opportunities that go beyond the buyer/seller relationship.

THE END OF TELEMARKETING

The use of referrals is growing partly because of the obstacles I've already mentioned: voice mail (high tech, but low touch), increased competition, and everyone being busier than ever before.

Now there's a new wrinkle in the marketing efforts of many businesses. It's called the National Do-Not-Call Registry. If this doesn't foreshadow the end of cold calling, I don't know what does. People are tired of cold calls coming into their homes (and businesses) at all hours. In the past year, a significant percentage of my seminar and consulting business has been devoted to companies that have traditionally relied on telemarketing to generate leads for their sales force. The do-not call registries (national and state) are slowly putting an end to this method of marketing. The great thing about switching

from a telemarketing-based business to a referral-based business is that you will become much more profitable because your cost-per-lead will drop to near zero. I will address the do-not-call regulations at length in Chapter 1.

SALES IS AN EVIDENCE BUSINESS

Our economy is fast becoming a service economy. Many salespeople are selling services instead of products. Those who are selling products are also selling *service* to help distinguish their products from their competitors'. When you have a product, it's usually something that people can touch, look at, sometimes hold, and watch it work before their eyes. Selling *service* is a much less tangible sale. Buyers understand what good service is, but they can't hold it in their hands or watch it work before they buy it.

When selling services (or the service support to your product), you must provide evidence that you will deliver on your promises. This is where the referral comes in. When a prospecting client meets you through a referral, the evidence level is already high. It's as if the referral source has testified on your behalf. This is why meeting you through a colleague or friend is their preferred method. Your buyers would rather meet you through a referral. The endorsement and testimony of others make them feel much more comfortable opening their door to you and giving you their business.

Get More Referrals Now!

PART ONE

THE FOUNDATION: ADOPT A REFERRAL MINDSET

Building a referral-based business is more than simply putting together a set of strategies and tactics. It's a way of thinking. It's a very specific style of doing business that begins with a commitment to building your business through relationships. Most salespeople and business owners *dabble* in referrals. They know what to do with one when they trip over it. But most salespeople and business owners do not have a *systematic approach* to making referrals happen on a regular and abundant basis. Therefore, this book begins with a discussion of some of the attitudes and habits of thinking that are necessary to successfully build your referral-based business.

Chapter 1

Do-Not-Call Lists—The Death of Cold Calling

"Cold calling is God's punishment for failure to get enough referrals."

My commitment to a referral-based business has changed the way I do business as well as my lifestyle—for the better. I no longer have to set aside time for cold calling or other less efficient marketing strategies. Using The Unlimited Referrals Marketing System®, I'm always asking for and getting referrals. Great referrals!

I began by "practicing" with my lower-level clients, before I approached one of my Top Five clients to ask for referrals. While it was clear that he didn't feel threatened, his response was, "I know a few people. Can I please get back to you on this?"

About 2 weeks later, this top client called me with a referral to one of his friends. I met with his friend and he became a multi-million dollar client.

AQUILES LARREA
NEW YORK, NY

In my book *Unlimited Referrals*, published in 1996, I predicted the "death of cold calling." It looks like my prediction is closer to coming true. On October 1, 2003, the national do-not-call list went into full effect. This list, resulting from broader telemarketing regulations (the Telephone Consumer Protection Act), is administered by both the Federal Trade Commission (FTC) and the Federal Communications Commission (FCC). The key objective of this national list is to prevent consumers from receiving unsolicited telemarketing calls. Companies are also required to maintain their own lists of consumers who do not wish to be called by their particular business. Companies engaged in telemarketing directly to consumers are expected to "scrub" (clean) their lists with the national list on a regular basis. Telemarketers are required to immediately acknowledge and record the names of people who request to be added to their own do-not-call list.

If you call consumers at their homes, and they are on the national do-not-call list (even from a referral) or on your own company's do-not-call list, you are subject to a penalty of $11,000 per violation. Now that's enough to put cold calling in the deep freeze!

While I'm writing this book, the national do-not-call list website is the most popular site on the Internet (in the United States). This number of names on the list is expected to exceed 60 million people. This sends a strong message to every business person and every salesperson. *People do not want to be cold called. Period.*

Although this do-not-call regulation only applies to calls to consumers, business people don't like to get cold calls either. Do you like getting cold calls? At home? At work? I rest my case.

Many states have created their own do-not-call lists as well. It is expected that most of these states will let their lists roll into the national list. As of this writing, Indiana has the steepest fine for calling someone on its list—$20,000 per violation. These do-not-call lists are frequently updated and are available to companies via the Internet.

While it's possible a consumer may opt not to register for a state or national do-not-call list and attempt to limit unwanted calls by getting on the lists of individual companies, many more consumers will opt to register for the lists, and then permit certain companies to call

them. If you've been given written permission by a consumer, you may call him or her for up to 3 months. You may also call consumers at home who are considered "customers" of your business. A "customer" is defined as a consumer with whom you have had some type of business transaction (purchase, service rendered, invoice paid, etc.) within the last 18 months.

As of this writing, not all telemarketing is prohibited by the do-not-call regulations. Most charities are exempt, as are calls for political fund-raising (why am I not surprised by this one?). In some states, certain companies may be allowed to solicit by telephone, but may be barred from using automated dialing systems. Before you or your employees pick up the phone to call consumers at their homes, make sure you are clear about the national and state regulations. Also, make sure you have access to these lists to compare your prospecting numbers with those that have been registered to prevent cold calling. Important: if you call consumers in their homes and they ask to be removed from your company's do-not-call list, comply immediately and hang up—and make sure your company maintains an up-to-date list.

Some consumers have become "citizen detectives." They are urged to register their homes on the do-not-call lists and file complaints. This is one of the strongest features of these laws. It gives registrants a course of action should telemarketers call illegally. To investigate a case, residents report violators by providing their name and/or the telephone number. While the FTC and FCC will not investigate every complaint—they are looking for repeated violations—salespeople and their companies are advised to operate within the constraints of these regulations.

When making calls directly to consumers, always identify yourself, your company, and the purpose of the call. For more information on do-not-call lists, go visit these websites: www.fcc.gov and www.ftc.gov.

WHAT DOES ALL THIS MEAN TO YOU?

You should make a commitment to building a referral-based business. Now! Your next great client wants to meet you through a referral, introduction, or recommendation from someone he or she already trusts.

This is a no-brainer, yet most small business owners and salespeople only dabble in referrals. This book should be your new sales bible, as it will give you the five skills you need to build a successful referral-based business. Using the strategies in this book, the do-not-call regulations will become a non-factor in your quest for new clients.

One of my clients had been extremely reliant on telemarketing. With the emergence of the do-not-call lists, his telemarketing efforts have become less productive, and as a result, his cost-per-lead has skyrocketed. After some training and consulting sessions with my company, Referral Coach International, he committed his company to building a referral-based business. He fired his entire telemarketing department. Really! Now here's the kicker—not only has he saved his company $400,000 per year, his sales have not dropped more than a few percentage points. Now *that's* results!

So, if you're not yet committed to building a referral-based business, I suspect you will be by the time you're done reading this book. Let's get to it.

Note: The do-not-call list applies to calls to consumers in their homes or on their cell phones. It does not apply to business-to-business calls. If you only call prospects at their place of business, you're still on safe ground—for now.

Any legitimate business that engages in some kind of telemarketing may register for access to the do-not-call list. The cost for this access will vary, depending on how many area codes you want access to. If you need access to five or fewer area codes, access to the list is free. The list is Internet based, so you can access it 24/7.

The "Safe Harbor" provision of the regulations allows for a company to make a reasonable mistake, as long as proper diligence is made to keep its list up-to-date. You are required to update your list on a quarterly basis. If you fail to update your list quarterly, the "Safe Harbor" provision will not protect you.

Please remember that I am not an attorney and you should not consider this legal advice. The regulations may also have been modified since the publication of this book. To ensure that your sales methods are in compliance with current laws, consult with a knowledgeable attorney before calling consumers in their homes or on their cell phones.

Chapter 2

Building Your Referral-Based Business

"Well begun is half done."

Your referral system is changing the way I do business—for the better. Over the past month I've been implementing your strategies and it's really paying off. Cold calling is as much fun as cleaning toilets in a sports stadium, and nobody likes to get cold calls anymore. With your referral system, I've been able to tap into my large client base and create a steady flow of high-quality referrals. I can't thank you enough!

John Koziol, CLU
Hockessin, DE

I have identified five critical skills to building a referral-based business.

SKILL 1—ADOPT A REFERRAL MINDSET

Your attitudes and assumptions toward referrals constitute the starting point toward building a successful referral-based business. You must adopt a *referral mindset*. Having this mindset means that you embrace referrals as the best way to build your business. When you have a referral mindset, referrals are not just something nice that happens every now and then. They are your primary method for acquiring new clients, or at least a major part of your overall marketing plan. When you truly adopt a referral mindset, everything you do in your business will promote your goal of getting more high-quality referrals.

SKILL 2—ENHANCE YOUR REFERABILITY

How do our clients say "thank you" to us? By coming back for more business and by referring others. This is the first cornerstone, because without it, other cornerstones will hardly be possible. You must serve your clients consistently well. Enough companies are providing such great service these days, so the service you provide will be measured by the high standards set by other companies—and not necessarily in your industry.

This section of the book will give you some ideas, as well as specific tools, you can immediately put to use to make sure you are serving your clients so well that they are ready to refer more business your way.

It's my belief that you should be getting referrals just by virtue of being in business. There are plenty of people who actually enjoy giving referrals and will do so without being asked. Even so, your service must "wow" people enough to get them talking. If you are not currently getting many referrals, you need to look at the service you provide and the relationships you establish with your clients.

SKILL 3—PROSPECT FOR REFERRALS

To achieve sustained success in sales, you must become a master prospector. A well-executed marketing plan will bring clients to your door (or phone). But that's not always enough. Sometimes the clients that come to you aren't always the clients you want. Sometimes the volume isn't enough to build to the level of sales you desire. You must always be proactive toward making referrals happen.

I'm really excited about this section of the book, because this is a topic about which very little has been written and taught to salespeople and small business owners. This section will teach you how to raise your referral gathering to a whole new level of success. Many people are great at serving clients, because that's the "safe" side of sales, but these same salespeople don't know how to leverage those great relationships into a continuous flow of new referral prospects. And as a result, so much money is left on the table.

SKILL 4—NETWORK STRATEGICALLY

Not all of your referrals need come from satisfied clients. Many can come from the relationships you nurture with people who may never become clients. Part Three of this book will help you identify the people who can give you a steady stream of quality referrals.

Networking is an overused term, not to mention a strategy at which few people are actually skilled. One reason why networking doesn't always produce the results people want is because they are not very strategic in their approach. Without a well thought-out strategy for networking, results are severely diminished.

SKILL 5—TARGET NICHE MARKETS

Creating a reputation for yourself and your company with a shotgun approach to marketing is very difficult. Narrowing your marketing focus to one or two well-defined niches makes it much easier to establish a reputation and will substantially increase your referral business.

When you target a niche, your real and perceived values are substantially increased. Plus, your requests for referrals are more targeted and therefore more effective. When you target a niche, you bring value to the first appointment that your non-targeting competitors can't bring. You can engage in a deeper level of conversation about the client's needs and wants right from the start.

Within a niche, your reputation will spread much faster than it could among diverse groups. This section will tell you everything you need to know to select and target a niche market. You will learn how to establish such a solid reputation in your target industry that prospects will be calling *you*. And if you call *them*, they likely will have heard great things about you already. Referrals will be generated so easily, in fact, that many will seem to come right out of the blue. You'll experience a constant flow of *found* business.

GET READY TO GET PICKY

An effective referral system can often attract more new business than you actually need—a good problem. For most salespeople and small business owners, the sales process reflects neediness. Because they don't have enough business coming their way, every new prospect takes on too much importance. This neediness increases the tension that already exists in the selling process and eventually hurts results. When you have an abundance of new business coming your way, not only will you be less needy in the sale, you can actually be selective and take on new clients who are a perfect fit for your business.

A COMPREHENSIVE APPROACH

Other books have been written on the subject of acquiring referrals; most only tackle networking and sometimes service. There is no book in existence, except the one you are holding in your hands, that offers such a comprehensive, step-by-step system for significantly increasing your sales by using referrals. Now let's get started building your successful referral-based business!

Chapter 3

The Relationship Is Everything

"The way of the world is meeting people through other people, and the referral is the warm way we get into their lives."

I think what makes your referral system work is that it's all about the relationship. Since I've adopted a referral mindset (that you taught me), I work extra hard to create relationships of value. The more value I bring to people, the more referrals I seem to get.

Gloria Mann
Richardson, TX

From the very first day I started selling, I knew intuitively that in sales, the relationships you establish with your prospects and clients are the basis for everything that gets accomplished. In my presentations to salespeople and business owners, I am always saying, "The relationship is everything!" As you begin to build your business from referrals, you must adopt the same attitude.

On the very first phone call to a prospect, it is the rapport you establish (the relationship) that allows the conversation to continue. It is the relationship that helps you feel more comfortable about asking probing questions. It is the relationship that allows you to have a longer conversation than you had expected. It is the quality of the relationship that develops that allows you to secure the appointment.

WORK TOWARD A PARTNERSHIP

During sales appointments, it is the growing relationship with your prospects that allows you to help them reveal their problems and share their goals and dreams. It is the relationship that allows you to discover with whom you are competing. It is the relationship that allows you to get a second appointment with more decision-makers. It is the relationship that gets you invited to their planning meetings. Whatever you are selling, and whatever the sell cycle, it is the relationship you establish that gives you influence with your prospect. Once your prospect becomes a client, the better the relationship you create, the more of a true partnership you will develop, as opposed to just a buyer/seller situation.

DON'T BE A VENDOR OR SUPPLIER

I hate the words *vendor* and *supplier*. Unless you are dealing with a purchasing agent who insists on using those words, I suggest you expunge them from your vocabulary. I prefer the word *partnership*. A *partner* is always interested in creating win/win situations—

where in every transaction both the buyer and the seller come out on top.

Without good relationships with prospects, clients, and referral alliances, you cannot produce an unlimited supply of referrals. Without quality relationships, referral marketing just won't work. And, of course, once you have quality relationships, you can leverage them into referrals.

Referral marketing is more than just a series of techniques. It is a philosophy, a way of doing business, a mindset that has relationships at its core. Create relationships—true business friendships—and each side of the partnership will continually work to serve the other.

Jim Cathcart, author of *Relationship Selling*, observes that all good salespeople have two traits in common: First, they love to make sales. In fact, they thrive on it. Second, and of equal importance, they respect their prospects and clients. These two qualities are the keys to success in relationship selling. As Jim says, "Selling should be a friendly act. Something we do to help people. Something we do with people and for people, not *to* them."

A NEW WAY TO SELL

Although most salespeople have changed with the times and have moved away from the old style of adversary selling, there are still remnants of this that show up in the language of sales. An example is the verb *close*. We use this word liberally to mean the completion of a sale. But is it really a close? *Close* implies an ending, and it implies something that we do *to* people rather than *for* them. What we are really trying to do is *confirm* the sale, *confirm* the relationship, and *confirm* the beginning of a partnership.

REFERRALS ELIMINATE TENSION IN THE SALE

One of the biggest obstacles to effective selling is tension between the buyer and the seller. Managing and controlling the tension level is one of the best ways a seller can increase the likelihood of a sale. When tension is up, cooperation is down. When tension is down, trust and cooperation begin to rise.

With a cold call, for example, when you contact most prospects, the tension level is high. They don't know who you are or why you are calling. They've probably had bad experiences with pushy salespeople, so you get a knee-jerk reaction that's not always pleasant. When you get together for an appointment, the buyers' tension level can continue to be high, because they want to make sure *they* make the decision to *buy*, as opposed to being *sold*. Your tension level starts to rise at this phase because you now have more at stake.

The tension level will ease a bit for both parties as you explore the relationship potential. But as the confirming stage draws near, if the tension has not been well managed, it will certainly increase for you, and probably for the buyer as well.

The great thing about referrals is that when a prospect comes to you through a referral, tension is usually very low if non-existent. Referral marketing leads to tension-free selling.

ACTIVE LISTENING IS THE KEY

We live in a society of poor listeners. Unfortunately, most salespeople and small business owners fall into this category. We are never taught how to listen effectively, despite the fact that well over half of human communication occurs through listening. We are taught how to read, write, and speak, but rarely how to listen. The most I ever heard my teachers in school say about listening was, "Class, listen!"

Listening is the most important relationship skill you can practice. It's a relationship skill because everyone needs to be listened to. Everyone! When you listen to someone actively with good focus, that person can feel it. To build trust and rapport with prospects, clients, and referral alliances, listen well. In addition to its relationship-building properties, listening helps you learn about your prospects,

clients, and referral alliances so you'll be in a stronger position to serve them. Without good listening habits, you will miss many opportunities to serve them and yourself.

Learn to Manage Your Distractions

Becoming a focused and active listener is mostly a matter of managing distractions. External distractions include such things as noise, ringing phones, a pretty woman or handsome man walking by, and a multitude of interruptions. Internal distractions include such things as preparing your response while the other party is still speaking, shutting down because you disagree with what the person is saying, and being preoccupied with judging the speaker based on his or her style, or accent, or clothing.

People usually talk at about 100 to 120 words per minute, but you can think at 400 to 500 words per minute. So, even if you are paying close attention, you still have tons of *free time* in your head. How you manage that free time will determine the quality of your listening, and ultimately the quality of the relationships you establish.

Become an Active Listener

My colleague, Dr. Tony Alessandra, is a successful author and speaker. He has written numerous books and tapes, including *The Dynamics of Effective Listening*, *The Platinum Rule*, and *Non-Manipulative Selling.* Tony says there are three types of listening dynamics: marginal, evaluative, and active listening.

Marginal Listening

These listeners may be guilty of:

- Being preoccupied with their own thoughts or feelings
- Distracting the speaker with nervous mannerisms
- Conveying a self-centered, arrogant attitude
- Misunderstanding much of what has been said
- Not even hearing what has been said

Here's an example of marginal listening:

CLIENT: You want me to take a whole day off from work so I can sit at home waiting for your repairman to show up?

CLIENT SERVICE REP: Our first available day is two weeks from Monday.

(Meanwhile, the CSR is thinking, "Just a half-hour to go before lunch.")

Evaluative Listening

Although better than marginal listeners, evaluative listeners still are not fully present. They are guilty of:

- Categorizing or evaluating what is said rather than trying to listen and understand
- Concentrating on composing a response
- Making quick judgments about the speaker
- Finishing the speaker's sentences
- Becoming distracted by emotionally-loaded words
- Rushing through the conversation

Evaluative listening sounds something like this:

CLIENT: You want me to take a whole day off from work so I can sit at home waiting for your repairman to show up?

CLIENT SERVICE REP (defensively): This is our busiest time of the year and there's nothing I can do about it.

Active Listening

Active listening takes desire and effort on your part. Active listeners:

- Concentrate on what people are saying

- Control their impulse to finish people's sentences (They are patient listeners.)
- Make an effort to see the speaker's point of view (They listen with empathy.)
- Give feedback to the speaker

Active listening leads to a sincere response like this:

CLIENT: You want me to take a whole day off from work so I can sit at home waiting for your repairman to show up?

CLIENT SERVICE REP: I can see how this may be a major inconvenience for you. Unfortunately, this is our busiest time of the year, and qualified technicians are hard to come by. Could you arrange for a neighbor to let our service person in?

It isn't enough to actively listen. We must *show* the speaker that we are listening. If we don't make that effort, the relationship value of our listening will be lost.

Active, focused listening is part of your attitude of service. It's a gift you give to others so that they will feel more comfortable with you. It's a gift that will pay you back many times over.

Chapter 4

Develop a Referral Mindset

"Leaving referrals to chance is a crime against your business."

ROY SHEPPARD

Your referral system has changed the way I think about my business. I've developed what you call a "referral mindset." The result has been more referrals from many different sources. I see opportunity I didn't see before. I act on that opportunity. I provide better service to my clients. I give referrals more often. I've formed "referral alliances." Referral success begins with your thinking and awareness.

FRED TERMAN
WHEATON, IL

If you want to build a referral-based business, you must look at how you think about referrals. If you want more referrals, you first have to expand your thinking. I call this a referral mindset. In this chapter I'll give you a checklist of items that make up a referral mindset. If these items reflect your thoughts and actions, you already have a strong referral mindset. As you read through each item, ask yourself, "Is this my thinking?" Also ask yourself, "Are my actions congruent with this thinking?"

REFERRAL MINDSET POP QUIZ

1. Yes / No I understand that my new clients *prefer to meet me through a referral* above any other way, so my primary method of acquiring new clients is through referrals.
2. Yes / No I understand referrals are the most *cost effective* method of building a business, so I enhance the profitability of my business by growing it mainly through referrals.
3. Yes / No Rather than just transactions, I look to the *lifetime value* of a client. I understand the lifetime value is not just the business a client will do with me, but the people that client will introduce me to over a lifetime.
4. Yes / No I have an attitude of *leverage.* As I enter into new relationships with prospects and clients, I'm constantly looking for ways to leverage the relationship to produce many win/win situations.
5. Yes / No I understand that I become more referable as I develop more trust with my prospects and clients, so I always strive to move beyond rapport and form *relationships based on strong mutual trust.*
6. Yes / No I look for *problems to solve.* Instead of selling products and services, I sell solutions to problems.
7. Yes / No I use a comprehensive and *systematic approach* to generating referrals in my business.

8. Yes / No I constantly look for *opportunities to ask* for referrals.
9. Yes / No I constantly look for *opportunities to give* referrals.
10. Yes / No I truly *expect* to get referrals from prospects and clients.

How did you do on the referral mindset pop quiz? Here's an explanation of each item and why it's so important to you.

1. I understand that my new clients *prefer to meet me through a referral* above any other way, so it's my primary method of acquiring new clients.

What happens when you're at home around dinner time and the phone rings, and the voice on the other end mispronounces your name and is obviously reading from a script? Are you excited about this cold call? Are you ready to give this stranger 20 minutes of your time? Of course not.

When I deliver seminars teaching my Unlimited Referrals Marketing System®, I always ask the participants, "Who likes to receive cold calls?" Rarely does a hand go up. (Except those occasional sadists who enjoy putting telemarketers through their paces.) Do you like to get cold calls? Of course not. Do your prospects? No!

How would someone prefer to be introduced to you and your business? Through a personal introduction, a recommendation, or a referral.

I'm not saying that cold calling shouldn't be a part of your tool kit. You should always be willing to get on the phone and call a good lead. If you're new in business, you probably need to generate activity just about any way you can. The goal, however, is to move away from cold calling as soon as possible.

I'm also not saying that seminar selling can't be a big part of your tool kit. Many businesses and top sales reps have great success with hosting educational seminars as a prospecting tool. Seminars, however, are expensive and risky. The cost-per-lead can be quite high, and it's not really how most people would prefer to be introduced to you and your business.

Cold calling, advertising, direct mail, and seminars can produce results, but usually by default. Prospects will respond to these forms of prospecting only when they don't have opportunities to meet you through referrals.

Here's the point. If the majority of your prospective clients would prefer to meet you through a referral, it must be your primary method of attracting them. You need to put yourself and your business in the flow of how people would like to meet you. As you put yourself in this natural flow, your business will grow more quickly and become more profitable.

2. I understand referrals are the most *cost effective* method of building a business, so I enhance the profitability of my business by growing it mainly from referrals.

What does it cost to put out an effective direct-mail campaign? What does is cost to put on a seminar? What does it cost to a salesperson's psyche to build a business through constant cold calling? Sure, these methods can produce results, but at what cost?

A key concept to remember in acquiring new business is the *cost-per-lead*. The more it costs you to acquire a lead, the less profitable your business will be.

Josh was introduced to me after one of my speeches as a "top producer" in his company. His numbers were impressive—to a degree. When I asked him how profitable his business was, he said, "Well, not as profitable as I'd like."

Through further discussion I discovered that his primary method of prospecting was a very sophisticated and impressive direct-mail system—and it did generate new business. Problem was his cost-per-lead was very high. Like cold calling, direct mail is mostly a numbers game. Once you know you have a good offer and a good system of delivering that offer, it all comes down to numbers. Mail enough pieces to the right people and you'll do some business.

Josh was mailing out thousands of pieces of mail per month—and spending thousands of dollars in the process. His cost-per-lead was too high! The result was a less profitable business.

That's the magic of having a solid referral system in place. Your cost-per-lead will be miniscule compared to direct mail, seminars, or virtually any other client-attraction method.

Remember: It's not how much you make. It's how much you *keep*. Using referrals as your primary client-attraction activity will put more money in your pocket.

3. Rather than just transactions, I look to the *lifetime value* of a client. I understand the lifetime value is not just the business a client will do with me, but the people that client will introduce me to over a lifetime.

About 12 years ago, I purchased a nice size permanent life insurance policy from Hal King, an agent I had met through a referral. About a year after the sale, Hal offered to take me to lunch to review the policy, and I accepted. He called it an "annual review." (By the way, the annual review is a common practice in the insurance business that can, and should, be translated into just about any business.)

At lunch, after we discussed my financial situation, Hal said (in a very weak way), "You don't happen to know anyone who's looking for life insurance do you?" (You see, Hal was fairly new in the business, and his "referred lead talk" needed a little work.) Of course I didn't know anyone looking for life insurance, but I gave him the names of three friends, and one of them actually became a client of Hal's.

Every year for 10 years, Hal took me to lunch to talk about my account as well as about referrals. Over those 10 years, I gave Hal a total of 43 referrals—21 of whom became his clients. I opened my Rolodex of business contacts to Hal. I opened my directory of speakers and seminar leaders to Hal. Why? Three reasons. 1) He stayed in contact with me in a way that kept him referable. That's important. 2) He asked for referrals. Do you think I would have given him 43 referrals if he hadn't asked? And 3) In the fifth year of our relation-

ship, Hal brought me four referrals. He had called these new prospects on my behalf, so they were expecting my call. Three out of the four became clients of mine. What happens when you give? You receive! The "law of reciprocity" kicked in, and I gave a ton back to Hal.

Man! Talk about a referral mindset! Hal has clearly tapped into the lifetime value of his relationship with me. Are you tapping into the lifetime value of your relationships with your clients?

The lifetime value of loyal clients is not just their repeat business. It's also their ability to connect you with who they know. Never forget that every client has the ability to lead you to other clients.

4. I have an attitude of *leverage*. As I enter into new relationships with prospects and clients, I'm constantly looking for ways to leverage the relationship to produce many win/win situations.

Do you have an attitude of leverage? Really? Some people get stuck on this word. They see leverage as some form of manipulation or "getting over" on someone. This is not what I mean at all. To me, leverage means creating a great relationship with a client (or friend, or center of influence), and then turning that relationship into something more than what had brought us together in the first place. It means taking a relationship that may have started with a transaction and turning it into a business friendship. It means constantly looking for opportunities to serve and be served, to help and be helped. That's leverage in the spirit of win/win. Of course, one of the "wins" for you can and should be quality referrals.

5. I understand that I become more referable as I develop more trust with my prospects and clients, so I always strive to move beyond rapport and form *relationships based on strong mutual trust*.

Trust is the grease of any relationship. It's the most basic element that determines the quality of a relationship. It is the same with referrals. As prospects and clients find you more trustworthy, they will be more willing to give you referrals.

How do you earn someone's trust? We could have a long discussion on this topic—it could be an entire book unto itself. But for

the sake of efficiency, let me distill it down to two main things you can attend to immediately.

- *Service.* We trust people who serve us well. We must go into our meetings with prospects and clients with an attitude of service. Before each meeting, we must stop and think, "How can I serve this person today?" And then we must do it. This builds trust, because the prospect or client sees we're not there to just sell them something. We are there to serve them. Professional speaker and colleague Joe Bonura says, "Stop calling yourself a salesperson. Think of yourself as a *serve person.* You're not there to sell, but to serve." When you serve your prospects, clients, and centers of influence, the referrals (and the sales) will come easily.
- *Do what you say you will.* I don't have to tell you that we live in a society where, more often than not, people don't follow through with their agreements. So, when we have a system in place that makes sure we do exactly what we said we would do—when we said we would do it—we really stand out. Thus, we build trust, because we can be counted on to deliver on our promises. Critical!

6. I look for *problems to solve.* Instead of selling products and services, I sell solutions to problems.

I sure hope you're not out there leading with products and services. I hope you're positioning yourself as a problem-solver. People don't look for a product for that product's sake. They're looking to solve a problem, prevent a problem, take advantage of an opportunity, or fulfill a desire—not just buy something. As I'm sure you've discovered, even when they are hunting for a specific product or service, they don't always know what they really need. Now it's your turn to ask some good questions. Do some "big picture" thinking. Listen to their *perceived* problems and desires, and then bring all your knowledge to bear on their situation.

This is the most powerful way to sell anything, and it makes you more referable early in the relationship.

7. I use a comprehensive and *systematic approach* to generating referrals in my business.

What happens when you don't have a systematic approach for acquiring new business through referrals? A couple of things: First, your business is unlikely to grow at a consistent and steady pace. If you're a sales rep, your production over a given time frame often looks like a roller coaster. This roller coaster production cycle often creates a great deal of unnecessary stress. Second, you don't always attract the type of clients you need to grow your business in the direction you desire. You may provide enough good service to create some word of mouth, which may drive some business your way. Even so, unless you have a proactive system for attracting the right clients to your business, you're likely to attract many prospective clients who aren't the type you really want. Working with "second tier" clients can bog down your business rather than nurture it.

A comprehensive and systematic referral process will help you create a situation where you may attract more qualified clients than you actually need. Why would you want such a situation? You will not operate your business coming from a place of *neediness* (not a strong place to be). Instead you will operate your business from a place of *abundance*. When you come from a place of abundance, your stress is reduced, and you can even become selective about whom you take on as a client. You can choose to do business with clients that will move your business forward and not bog you down. You will no longer have to spend your time with clients who are too time consuming, who drive you crazy, and who are simply no fun.

This book teaches you The Unlimited Referrals Marketing System®, a comprehensive and systematic approach to referrals.

8. I constantly look for *opportunities to ask* for referrals.

One part of this system teaches that you must be willing to ask for referrals. In Part Three, we'll address the skill of asking for referrals. This book, unfortunately, can't give you the *will* to do it. That's something you need to develop on your own. I hope this book will inspire you to consistently ask for referrals.

In the life insurance business, you hear the common phrase "referred lead talk." This is a talk you're prepared to have with virtually any prospect or client when it's time to request referrals. When you have a good referred lead talk that has truly become a habit, your confidence soars, and your actions are more effective.

9. I constantly look for *opportunities to give* referrals.

There is no better way to send the message to the world that you work from referrals than by giving referrals. Become a resource for your clients by being a connector of people. Later in the book, I'll tell you everything you need to know about how to give referrals in a way that brings them back to you many-fold. But don't wait until you read that chapter. Start today by looking for opportunities to give referrals to your prospects, clients, and anyone else in your life. Give and ye shall receive!

10. I truly *expect* to get referrals from prospects and clients.

When I met Jerry, he had been a life insurance agent for 18 months and he was out-producing many of the veterans in his office. He had qualified for the prestigious Million Dollar Round Table in his second year, an accomplishment that was relatively rare for someone in the business for such a short time. And, he had achieved all this without making any cold calls after his first few months. He did it with referrals from prospects and clients.

I invited Jerry to lunch to learn what he was doing so I could teach it to you. We talked about many things, but two main points came out in our conversation.

First, Jerry made sure he became referable as soon as possible in his new relationships. He did his best to let his prospects know he wasn't there to sell them anything, but that he was just there to help them. He asked good questions, he listened well, and he provided the perfect advice for the client's situation. Through this behavior Jerry earned trust and provided an experience his prospects and clients wanted to share with others.

Second, Jerry *expected* to get referrals. He had an attitude of expectation that went something like this: "I expect people to like me.

I expect to discover their real need and only sell them exactly what they need when they need it. I expect to give them an experience they want to share with others. I expect my prospects and clients to give me referrals."

Jerry's attitude of expectation led him to behave in certain ways that increased his chances of getting referrals. How about you? Do you expect the referral process to take hold, or do you just wish and hope for it to happen? There's a huge difference. When you expect referrals, your awareness changes. With your new awareness, your opportunities for more effective action increase as well.

I think you can see that if the first nine items of the referral mindset are in place, you can easily *expect* to get referrals. The first nine feed into this attitude of expectation.

THE BEST WAY TO BUILD YOUR BUSINESS

Having a referral mindset means that you have accepted the notion that the best way to build your business is by generating referrals. Referrals are not just something nice that happens every now and then; they are your primary method for acquiring new clients. When you truly adopt a referral mindset, you will see opportunities for referrals you might not have noticed before. When you truly adopt a referral mindset, everything about your marketing, sales, and service processes will be geared toward creating a steady supply of high-quality referrals.

I've observed in life that the more powerful our thinking, the more powerful our actions. The more you can embrace a referral mindset, the more the referral process is always in your awareness, and the more you turn this thinking into action, the more you can create a true referral explosion.

Building a Referral-Based Business Is More Important Than Ever Before

(Inspired by the writing of Roy Sheppard, author of *Rapid Results Referrals*—Centre Publishing, 2001)

- Unlike advertising and other marketing initiatives, your results from a referral program can be easily tracked and verified.
- A referral program yields the best marketing investment possible.
- Referrals help reduce your marketing costs in times of economic uncertainty.
- Each time you receive a referral, your client is telling you that you're doing a good job.
- Delighted clients who become advocates are the best sales force a company can have.
- Each time a client gives you a referral, you have a chance to make them look like a hero.
- When you have created a self-perpetual flow of referrals, you eliminate the anxiety of wondering from where future business will come, and you can be more picky about who you take on as a client.
- Due to do-not-call registries, caller ID, and electronic screening, cold calling has been rendered almost completely ineffective.
- Clients reduce their risk of making a bad decision when they "buy" from referrals.
- A voice-mail message to a new prospect is most likely to be returned if it comes from a referral.
- A claim by a third party carries much more credibility than if you were to make the claim yourself.
- Prospects obtained through referrals give you fewer objections because they trust you more.
- Growing a business through referrals is the most fun.

PART TWO

THE FIRST SKILL: ENHANCE YOUR REFERABILITY

The referral process cannot happen if you and your business are not referable. You and your business become referable when you provide your clients with a memorable experience. You remain referable when you maintain superior service and form quality relationships. In most businesses, that memorable experience is brought about by the *process* through which you bring your prospects and clients. The better the process, the more referable you become early in the relationship. The higher the level of service you provide to your clients, and the better the relationships you form, the more likely you will remain referable throughout the lifetime of the relationship.

The bottom line to providing great service and forming great relationships is that you must truly care about your clients. You must be fully committed to delivering first class products, processes, and service. You must *want* to do it. You must have an attitude of service for your clients. An attitude of service is almost impossible to teach. You either have it or you don't. For referral marketing to work for you, you must strengthen your attitude of service.

Shep Hyken, my colleague and expert on service, says, "Going the extra mile does not necessarily mean a lot of extra effort. It just requires caring and thinking about the needs of your clients; knowing your business and anticipating their needs and potential problems."

Chapter 5

Exceed Your Clients' Expectations

"Your clients are happy when you meet their expectations. Your clients become loyal when you continually meet and exceed *their expectations. Your clients become word-of-mouth machines when you create memorable experiences."*

Now that I've decided to build a referral-based business, I've found that the service I provide to my customers is better than ever before. Not only am I trying to retain them as customers, I'm also trying to leverage their loyalty into introductions. It's working. Last month I brought in 10 new customers from referrals—a record for our business.

ANDREW HAWKINS
LOS ANGELES, CA

To begin building your referral-based business, you must start with the service you provide to your clients and the relationships you form. A number of years ago I read the results of a study that determined that clients who do not rate you as "completely satisfied" (not mostly or fairly) are candidates to take their business elsewhere. This certainly makes sense. I'm sure you patronize businesses with which you are not completely satisfied, yet you continue to give them your business. However, when an alternative comes along, you're usually willing to explore that option. True for you? This is also true for your clients.

A simple example of exceeding client expectations happened to me while in the middle of writing this book. Over one weekend, while doing some work on my house and yard, I had to patronize three large do-it-yourself home centers. I was in a hurry, so in each case I stopped a floor person (I hesitate to call them sales or client service people) for assistance. What did I expect? I expected them to politely tell me exactly where the item that I wanted was located.

At the first store, the floor person wasn't quite sure of the answer, so he gave me some vague point and mumble. This didn't meet my expectations, and I left with a bad feeling about the store. At the second store, the floor person pointed to the aisle and said, "It should be somewhere on aisle D. If it's not there, try the end of aisle E." Then he went on his way. This was better, but I still had to wander around for a long time before I finally found the item—at the very end of aisle F.

At the third store (this is beginning to remind me of the three little pigs and the big bad wolf), not only did the floor person know exactly where the item was, but he stopped what he was doing and walked me to the spot. This exceeded my expectations. I was a happy wolf. Now I shop there most often, even going out of my way on occasion to do so.

As another illustration of superior service, let me introduce you to Margaret. Margaret is a financial advisor with American Express Financial Advisors. Margaret truly has an attitude of service.

Whenever she refers a client to another professional, such as an accountant or attorney, she accompanies the client to the first meeting. Her attitude of service has paid off; Margaret is a top producer.

WHAT DO YOUR CLIENTS EXPECT?

Before you can meet and exceed your clients' expectations, you must know what those expectations are. Do you know what your new prospects and clients expect from you? How do you know this? Have you asked them?

One of the most important things you can do to become referable quickly in a relationship is talk to your prospects and clients about what they expect from you. Make a habit of asking them this. Make a habit of finding out how they've been served in the past by the same or similar businesses. Make a habit of asking them why they are contemplating switching to you. Here's a great question to ask a new prospect or client very early in the relationship: "Let's pretend it's 2 years (or whatever time frame fits your business) from today, and we've been working together for that time. How will we know we've been successful? What's your measure of our success in working together?" Now be quiet and let them tell you.

When you ask these types of question, you not only learn what they expect, you also help to build trust. Trust is critical to the referral process. Trust is not easy to build quickly. Discussing expectations early and often in the relationship will help you build trust.

It is important to remember that people's perceptions and expectations about good service and quality business relationships are constantly changing. As your clients move from one buying experience to another, they experience different types and levels of service. Their future expectations will typically be based upon the best experience they've had in the past. This means that the bar designating what your clients expect from you is constantly being raised—by other companies providing products and services that may be totally unrelated to your business.

Your clients can be a part of your sales force, and you don't have to pay them a dime in commissions. You just have to *wow* them as often as you can.

Client service expert Barbara Glanz developed a helpful distinction that she calls the "human-business model." She observes that in every business interaction we have, something is happening simultaneously on two levels: the *human level* and the *business level*. The business level gets the work done, while the human level is all about how the participant feels about the interaction. The client's experience is the combined result of both the business and the human levels of the interactions. Clients want their business needs met while being treated with respect, friendliness, and empathy.

Let's say you go into a discount appliance store to buy a new television. You find the model you want at the price you want, but the salesperson is a little obnoxious and not very helpful. Do you buy the TV? Probably. Do you refer other people to the store? Maybe. Do you refer others to that salesperson? Definitely not. Sometimes the human side of the equation won't prevent the sale, but more often than not, it will decrease the likelihood of repeat business and kill the possibility of referrals.

Your clients will refer others to you if they like you and trust you. You create this dynamic by being trustworthy, providing a valuable process followed up with superior service, and always working to strengthen your client relationships.

Chapter 6

Put Your Attitude of Service into Action

"Those who fail, fail to follow through."

We've implemented a "referral culture" in our business. Every employee—from top to bottom—knows that we want our customers talking about us to others. We know we'll be most profitable when we grow through referrals and word of mouth. Every month we meet to discuss how we can make our business more referable.

Brett Johnson
Ellicott City, MD

Your *attitude* of service becomes a *commitment* to service when you put it into action. Are you truly committed to your career as a professional salesperson or small business owner? If so, client retention must be among your top priorities. It's one thing to win a client's business the first time, but it's quite another thing to keep that business for years to come. If your clients are not coming back for more, you are definitely not creating a situation where they will give you referrals.

TURN YOUR ATTITUDE INTO ACTION

Almost every business (although not all) has a repurchase cycle. Most people buy a new car within 3 to 5 years; a new copier every 2 to 3 years; a new computer every 2 to 3 years; and so on. Cycles vary, but most industries have them. Yours may be more or less frequent.

For example, if you sold someone an item to give as a birthday or an anniversary gift, you should call that person about 330 days later for the next opportunity to serve him (have your computer remind you and generate an e-mail message to him). If you served that person well the first time, maintained his contact information in an organized database, and perhaps stayed in touch in a simple way, your contact will be well received, even appreciated.

The point is that if you are in it for the long haul, you will do what it takes to make sure your clients come back to you for more. If you want to create a referral explosion, then you must also focus on creating repeat business.

YOUR INTEGRITY WILL BE TESTED

In business, integrity means two things: First, it means doing what you say you will do. Second, it means never violating your own standards of behavior.

Every time you tell a prospect or client that you will do something, you'd better do it—in a timely fashion. This is the foundation on which trust is built. Let your prospects and clients know from the

very beginning that your word means something. Show them they can count on you to do exactly what you say you will do. This is not always an easy standard to uphold. Often we agree to something without thinking it all the way through, only to realize later that we misjudged our ability to deliver on our promise.

Be careful about what you say you will do. Be thoughtful with how you give your word. Take an extra moment to look at your schedule or think the situation all the way through. My clients have become accustomed to me making careful decisions, and since I follow through on my word, they appreciate my thoughtfulness. If you say you will have a project done by 4 p.m. on Monday, get it done by that time. If there is a good reason why it won't be done by then, don't wait for the client to call you. Call him as soon as you know there will be a delay. Keeping promises is essential to maintaining your integrity and building trust—and earning referrals. I guarantee that if the commitment time passes and you don't call, he will remember it. He'll withhold his trust until you prove yourself.

The second aspect of integrity has to do with your word to yourself. A person with integrity never engages in behavior that goes against his or her own standards. The vast majority of your clients will respect and trust you when they see that you have high standards for yourself, even when that means not giving them exactly what they want every now and then.

Don't get me wrong; you need to be infinitely flexible in how you serve your clients. No service policy should be written in stone. Still, your personal standards should never be violated. True, you may lose a client who asks you to do business in a way that violates your personal standards, but compromising on what you hold important does not allow for a win/win relationship. Every sale must be a win for both you and your client. Clients who don't let you have your half of the equation are not good clients. (Yet, there may be times when you are willing to "lose" on a particular deal so that you can get a "win" later on.) Setting your personal standards for business (and the rest of your life) is an ongoing process. Sometimes we aren't even aware of a standard until it is tested.

Integrity is your foundation for creating trust with your clients, not to mention everyone else in your life. When people talk about you behind your back, you want them to say, "I can count on her," or "He's a man of his word."

The following are some steps you can take to demonstrate your integrity and commitment to service.

Tell the Truth

Never lie to a client. Keeping track of the truth is hard enough. With that said, knowing *when* to tell the truth under certain circumstances is something of an art form. Situations may arise in which the client does not need to know every detail all at once. When all is said and done, tell the truth to your clients.

Thank Your Clients Often

Almost every business person I meet knows about the value of sending a thank you note after making a sale or performing a service, yet most business people are not in the habit of doing this. This gesture alone will help you to stand out in a crowded marketplace. How many thank you notes did you send out last year? Send out twice as many this year.

Show Your Appreciation

You can show your appreciation to your clients in many other ways.

Many business people like to keep a steady stream of ad specialties flowing to their clients: mugs, pens, sticky-notes, and the like. I suggest you look for even more creative ways to use ad specialties as part of your appreciation mix. After all, something with your logo on it is not really a gift. It's an ad promoting your business.

I know of one company that sends inspirational poems mounted in walnut frames to their clients every year at Thanksgiving. As they count their blessings, their clients are among them. Client appreciation events are great ways to express your appreciation. Invite your

clients to group dinners, sporting events, boat rides, and the like. Building this type of relationship with your clients shields them from the competition.

Instead of reserving all your special discounts and promotions for new clients, why not offer added service or special discounts for your existing clients? If you aren't your company's top executive, persuade her to visit some of your most valued clients, just to reinforce your entire company's appreciation of their business. Have her bring along a thank you card signed by the employees.

Deliver Superior Internal Client Service

You already know that you have external clients, but have you thought about who your internal clients are? Every employee of a business is there to serve the clients. If they are not serving the clients directly, then they are serving someone who is serving the clients. These internal relationships usually work in two ways. They are *your* clients because they deliver goods, services, or information to you so that you can better serve the external clients. You are *their* client because you have to deliver information to them so that they can do their jobs most efficiently and effectively.

Client service expert Barbara Glanz says, "It is a lot easier to create loyal external clients if the organization's internal clients are cared for and supported. Research shows that the way an organization's internal clients are treated is ultimately the way an external client will be treated."

Glanz goes on to say, "Employee loyalty also has an impact on client loyalty. Have you ever been in an organization where people really seemed to enjoy their work? Chances are they are well treated as internal clients, and this makes them feel good and makes them better able to serve the external client as well."

So, consider these questions: Have you (and your company) identified all your internal clients? Do you sit down together on a regular basis to discuss how you can better serve each other so that your external clients are served impeccably?

Clarify, Don't Assume!

When clients give you "fuzzy phrases," don't assume you understand. Clarify. When clients say they need something "as soon as possible," stop and find out exactly what that means to them. When clients say "we want the highest quality," do you know what "high quality" means to them? When internal clients say "I'll try," get them to make a time-frame commitment.

Know Your Competition

Knowing your competition well not only gives you a selling advantage early on, it continues to help you serve and sell to your client throughout the relationship. You should always serve your clients with the knowledge that they are your competitors' prospects.

Do you know what pressures—internal or external—your clients are under to move their business? Do you know what they say to all those other salespeople? If you don't, I suggest you get to know your clients better and find out. The more you know about your competition, the more you can do to make sure you are always the better choice.

Your clients may not use you for all the products or services you provide. Do you know who else they are using and why? Do you know what they like and dislike about them? There is a great deal you can learn from this, and you may also find opportunities to increase the percentage of the business your clients do with you.

Record Every Service Transaction

Most effective salespeople document their prospecting efforts. They keep track of every contact and conversation. Most salespeople, however, stop there. They don't usually keep good documentation going once the sale has been made. I know a sales rep for a building contractor who uses his laptop computer to keep a running log of every job. Every time something happens, he puts it into this document. This helps him keep track of the job, and it comes in handy if a problem arises.

Are you keeping track of all your client interactions? How can you apply this strategy to your situation?

Never Tell Clients They Are Wrong

We all know the client is not always right, but we have to be very careful how we let them know that. I once took some negatives to a photo lab to be turned into prints. There were about 20 different negatives, so the order was a little complicated. I read off the numbers I wanted printed to the store clerk and she recorded them. When she read the order back to me, it was not what I had wanted. She immediately told me, in an accusatory tone, that I had given her the wrong numbers. Of course, I became mildly angry.

The truth of the matter is that I may have made a mistake. We'll never know for sure. Even so, when she accused me of the error, she damaged her and the lab's relationship with me. I may go back to that lab in spite of her, but certainly not because of her.

Be very careful how you let clients know they've made a mistake. Take as much on yourself as possible first, and when you do have to tell them, do it in a teaching manner—not arrogantly or patronizingly—but from a place of genuine care and concern.

Chapter 7

Make Your Clients Go "Wow"

"Client satisfaction is the gap between what the client expects and what they get."

Your referral system has made us realize that client satisfaction is not enough. We have to "wow" our clients if we are going to get them talking about us. Since bringing in new customers from referrals is more cost effective, we reward our employees—financially—every month when we make our referral goals.

TERRIE LAWSON
SEATTLE, WA

TIME-TESTED IDEAS

There are many things you can do to exceed your clients' expectations and enhance your referability. Exceeding expectations is a function of your desire and your creativity. Be creative in how you serve your clients, and they will spread the word to others. Here are some time-tested ideas. Use as many as you can.

Call Clients with Status Reports

Depending on your type of business, you may have opportunities to call your clients between the time they place the order and the time you deliver it. Schedule one or more status report calls (or e-mails) to let your clients know that everything is on schedule. They will appreciate you checking on their order or project, and everyone appreciates a "good news" call.

Always "Install" Your Product or Service

Sales expert and author Jim Cathcart says, "The most successful salespeople don't just sell their product or service. They install it after the sale. No matter what your line of business, devise a way to make your client feel comfortable with the product or service after the sale." Cathcart offers the following examples for installing a product or service:

1. If you sell residential real estate, give each buyer an owner's manual for the new home. Show buyers where the gas, water, and electric switches and meters are. Prepare a list of important phone numbers for their neighborhood. Give them a map that shows nearby schools, churches, and stores. (If you focus on a well-defined geographic area, this is easier than it might seem.)
2. If you sell automobiles, take time to show the buyer how to operate the new car. Go over the manufacturer's manual, and be willing to answer questions.

3. If your product is clothing, show the client how to use accessories with it to create a different look.
4. If you sell insurance, prepare a summary emphasizing that this isn't a one-time purchase, and that as their insurance needs change over time you'll be there to provide guidance and suggest any necessary adjustments.

"The key to continued success," Cathcart concludes, "is showing the client how to maximize the use of whatever was purchased."

If you sell an ongoing service, such as financial planning, printing, bookkeeping, or temporary employment services, introduce clients to people in your office with whom they are likely to come in contact. Your clients will be more comfortable and trusting each time they call a member of your team.

Be Careful How You Turn Clients Over to "Customer Service"

First of all, it's my feeling that everyone in your company is part of your "client service" department. Everyone should be ready, willing, and able to speak to clients and satisfy their needs as best they can. Since every client has the potential to lead many more clients to your business, you should always welcome opportunities to serve your client long after the sale has been made. Even if your company has a client service department, be careful how you turn your clients over to it.

Several months ago I switched my long-distance telephone service to a small company that had great rates. The salesperson was terrific at showing me how I'd benefit from his service. I was happy with the prices he quoted and with his initial service, so when he asked me for referrals, I gave him three. A month later, I began to have problems with the calling-card feature of the service. When I called the salesperson, he acted as if he couldn't be bothered and said that I needed to talk to "customer service." This left me feeling burned. I'll never recommend this service to anyone else because the salesperson betrayed my trust, and since the problem has yet to be resolved, I'm about to switch my service again.

Maintain Good Relationships with Your Vendors

Barbara Collins is the owner of Barbara's Image Boosters, an ad specialty business. She says, "In this business, normal production time is 4 to 6 weeks for many items. But I've built relationships with factories that meet rush demands. A client may call me in desperation because he needs something for a trade show in a few days. Because of the relationships I've nurtured, I can usually find something and have it in his hands the day he needs it." Foster partnerships with vendors that can help you look like a hero to your clients.

Get to Know Your Clients Better

Whenever possible, get to know your clients beyond what brought you together in the first place. Form business friendships with as many clients as you can. Get to know them as people. Take a genuine interest in them. Not every client wants you to do this, but most will appreciate it.

The clients who give me the best referrals, and continue to give me referrals long after I've served them, are those I now count as business friends. If your attitude is strictly business, you are probably missing tons of opportunities for referrals, not to mention more business from your existing clients.

Bottom line: Creating business friendships increases client loyalty and enhances your referability.

Get to Know Your Clients' Companies

Get to know your clients in ways that go beyond what you sell. Find out what their business goals are. Find out what problems they are having in areas that, at first glance, have little or nothing to do with what you sell. This will help you serve them in many ways over time. You will become a much more valuable resource, and you can even occasionally provide them with other resources.

If you sell printing and you view yourself as merely a vendor or supplier, you may never get to know your clients well. If you see yourself as a partner who is not just selling print services but who is also helping them communicate information, you will get to know them much more deeply, and you will be in a position to create many more win/win situations. This principle can be applied to any business.

Help Your Clients Really Know Your Company

Don't become pigeonholed. Your clients first started doing business with you based on their need at the time. Even though you told them about the full range of services you offer, all they probably saw was the specific product or service that would help them with that specific need. You serve your clients better when you keep them informed of everything you offer. If you sold them life insurance, make sure they know that you also handle disability insurance and other financial services. If you sold them two-color printing, make sure they know you can print four-color as well. If you've created a good working relationship, clients will thank you for reminding them of other ways you can help make their life easier.

Find Ways to Compliment Your Clients

I like to buy nice suits at a great price. I shop in a little store that is attached to the factory where the suits are made. If I don't like anything hanging on the rack, the salesperson will go into the plant to see what's being worked on that day. Because this factory is more than an hour from my home, I take the suits I buy to a local tailor to have them fitted. The last time I bought a suit this way, I was reminded of the value of complimenting the client in any way you can.

I was trying on the suit. As the tailor, an elderly Italian gentleman, measured me he said, "This is a nice-a suit. Where you get-a this suit?" I told him. He then said, "This a nice-a suit. I gonna take-a my time with this-a suit." I felt great. When I bought the suit, I thought it was nice. Now my opinion was validated by an Italian tailor. Wow!

A week later, I went in to pick up the suit. When I tried it on, he moved it around a little. Then he said, "This a nice-a suit. Where you get-a this suit?" I told him. He said again, "This a nice-a suit. I took-a my time with this-a suit." I felt great again. Maybe he says this to everyone, but maybe not. He liked my suit. I liked him. That's the way this concept works.

Keep Serving Your Clients After the Sale

Since you know that every client you serve is connected to other potential clients, you want to keep finding opportunities to serve them, even in ways that have nothing to do with your specific business. Lynne Smith, a marketing consultant, tells a story that illustrates this point perfectly. "After completing a project for Client A in San Francisco, I provided something extra by sending him a list of resources directly related to his additional needs. He was so appreciative of the extra service I gave him that he referred me to Client B in Atlanta, who referred me to Clients C and D. Client C has referred me to Client E in Denver and Client F in Galveston, Texas. This is the story that never ends." As well it shouldn't, I might add.

By doing a little something extra for one client, Lynne created a chain reaction that may never stop. That's the power of great service coupled with a referral mindset. The result: a referral explosion.

Survey Your Clients Over the Phone

You should be constantly asking your clients, "How am I doing?" and "If we could do one thing better, what would it be?" More importantly, you should be asking these questions over the phone—not in writing. Here are six reasons to conduct your client surveys over the phone:

1. You obtain more useful information—it's easier to talk than it is to write.

2. You demonstrate how much you care about serving them well.
3. You obtain more honest information—it's easier to "open up" over the phone than in person.
4. Your response rate will be much higher—close to 100 percent.
5. This is another personal contact with your clients.
6. You can communicate feelings and intentions much better in a conversation than you can in writing.

Marketing genius Jay Abraham says that to lift yourself and your company above the competition:

> You cannot service too much.
>
> You cannot educate enough.
>
> You cannot inform too much.
>
> You cannot offer too much follow-up and follow through too far.
>
> You cannot make ordering too easy.
>
> You cannot make calling or coming into your place of business too desirable.

Though we might debate some of these points if we take them apart, I think you can understand the spirit of what he's saying. These are things we must do to gain and keep clients, and it's especially important now that we realize that every client can lead us to others.

WHAT'S THE PAYOFF?

In this chapter, I hope I demonstrated that providing exceptional service to your clients will come back to you many fold in referrals, as well as increased business from them. The better you serve your clients and prospects, the better their referrals will be, and the easier it will be to convert those referrals into new clients.

Sometimes the Little Things Are the Big Things

- Stretch. If you paint houses for a living and your client needs the name of a good roofer, find him one. If he is staying at your hotel and his car gets a flat, change it. Help your client.
- Don't charge for "extra" services when you don't need really need to. Be your client's business friend. Don't worry. You'll more than make up the money in future business and referrals.
- Don't just be there for them from 9 to 5. Hand-write your cell phone number on your business card as you give it to them. They'll likely never use it unless they really need to, but it reassures them.
- Keep your word. Doing what you're supposed to do when you are supposed to do it is the very minimum required to provide good client service and generate referrals.
- When something goes wrong—and it will—apologize. When you apologize, you're not admitting fault, you're just sorry your client is being inconvenienced. This reduces tension because it demonstrates that you are there for them. (Almost no one in business ever says they're sorry.) Then, immediately after you apologize, fix the problem as quickly as possible.
- Set high service standards for yourself and your company—and tell your clients about them.
- If clients stop doing business with you, don't burn your bridges. Go out of your way to make them feel comfortable about coming back.
- Compromise with a smile. If you decided to give the client what he or she wants, even if it's not a win for you, give in completely and cheerfully. Don't make the client feel guilty. Guilt doesn't create client loyalty or bring about referrals.
- Help your clients understand your business. Teach them the best ways and times to interact with your business to maximize their satisfaction. Explain your systems and why they are best for the client, as well as you.
- Say "thank you" every time you get the chance.

Chapter 8

The Value of the Complaining Client

"A relationship that's had a problem handled well is a stronger relationship than one that's never had a problem."

I always felt uncomfortable when my customers complained. Then I took your advice and always started my response to their complaint with "I'm sorry." I'm still amazed at how well it works. People don't expect it. I guess they expect me to get defensive. I just tell them I'm sorry for their inconvenience (regardless of who caused it), and then try to find a solution that will make them happy. It's such a simple, yet powerful idea. Thank you!

Marty Rosenberg
Owings Mills, MD

Marketing and service expert Theodore Levitt says, "One of the surest signs of a bad or declining relationship is the absence of complaints from the client. The client is either not being candid or not being contacted. Probably both. The absence of candor reflects the decline of trust, the deterioration of the relationship."

A study performed by The Technical Assistance Research Programs Institute based in Washington, D.C., revealed some interesting findings. How do they apply to *your* business?

- For big-ticket durable goods, 40 percent of unhappy clients won't complain.
- For medium-ticket durable goods, 50 percent of unhappy clients won't complain.
- For big-ticket services, 63 percent of unhappy clients won't complain.
- For small-ticket services, 55 percent of unhappy clients won't complain.

This study also discovered that complainers are more likely to continue doing business with the company that upset them than non-complainers.

The Strategic Planning Institute of Cambridge, Pennsylvania, conducted a similar study that revealed more relevant information:

- The average business never hears from 96 percent of its unhappy clients.
- Of clients who register a complaint, 70 percent will do business with the company again if the complaint is resolved.
- Of clients who have a complaint, 95 percent will do business again if the problem is resolved quickly.

These studies confirm what I've believed for a long time:

1. Many people don't like to complain about the little stuff that didn't meet their expectations.
2. It's important that you encourage your clients to complain.

GET YOUR CLIENTS TO COMPLAIN

"Why would I want them to complain?" you might ask. "Complaints are not much fun." You want your clients to complain for at least four reasons:

1. If they don't complain, you won't know their problems and can't fix them.
2. If one client is having a problem, then it's quite likely that others are having it as well. You may need to fix your systems and/or policies.
3. Research indicates that if clients don't complain, they are likely to quietly go to your competition—and they certainly won't give you any referrals.
4. Unhappy clients usually tell many other people about their bad experiences.

I challenge every salesperson, small business owner, and company executive: *Get your clients to complain!* Sure, complaints can be downright tough to handle sometimes, but complaining clients are valuable to you and your business.

You must be willing to be "in the complaint." I once heard it expressed as being willing to "put your head in the lion's mouth." If you just sense your client is not happy with something, don't stick your head in the sand and hope the problem will go away. It *will* go away—*along with the client.* Be willing to step into the problem and be there for your clients. Walter Winchell once said, "A true friend is someone who walks in when others walk out." That's true of business friends as well.

HIT THE "JACKPOT"

My friend Gary Glaser is the sales manager at a printing company in Pennsylvania. As you might imagine, there are plenty of problems and complaints to be found in his industry. But Gary refers to problems as "jackpots," because he believes inherent in each problem is the opportunity to increase client loyalty and thus increase business.

When clients see that you are there for them during problems, they value the depth of the relationship you are able to offer. As a result, their loyalty, public praise, and referrals increase. Also, quite often when there is a problem, higher-ups from the organization get involved in finding the solution. This is an opportunity for you to meet other influencers in the organization that can lead to more business from them. Problems and complaints are truly jackpots!

WHAT TO DO WHEN SOMEONE COMPLAINS

Here are my eight steps for handling a complaining client:

1. Say "I'm sorry." These should be the first words out of your mouth. It costs nothing. It isn't admitting fault. You're just sorry that they are feeling inconvenienced. These are the most powerful words you can speak to a complaining client. Saying "I'm sorry" right from the get-go can even keep people from becoming angry.
2. Don't take it personally and get defensive. If you do, you're likely to make excuses, challenge their perceptions, and point fingers at others. All of these accomplish nothing, and they make your clients feel as if you don't really want to be there for them.

   You may do this without even realizing it. Has anyone ever complained to you about something in which you had little or no involvement? Were the first words out of your mouth, "I'm sorry this has happened. Let's see what I can do to help," or were they something like, "Well, that's not something I had anything to do with, but I'll check into it for you?" You think you're being helpful, but the first message that comes across to your client is "I'm protecting myself first."
3. Don't argue. Nobody has ever won an argument with a client. Even if you "win" and prove you are right, you lose. Don't worry so much about who is right and who is wrong—find a solution to the problem.
4. Demonstrate your willingness to be involved in the problem and work hard to find a solution. Offer your help in a tone of voice that matches their level of concern. If they are getting angry, let them talk as much as possible. Don't get angry back, and don't go away. Just be there for them.

5. Establish the facts. If your client is angry, be a good listener. This lets him or her blow off steam, and it helps you establish the facts as best you can. You may need to talk to some of your internal clients to verify the facts. This will help to minimize a client's tendency to exaggerate. It will also help you resist the temptation to admit the fault of the company (or someone within the company) until you know all the facts.
6. Resolve the problem quickly. Studies indicate that the faster you resolve problems, the less damage is done, and the more likely your clients will stick with you.
7. Thank clients for bringing their concern to your attention. This lets them know that you value their complaints, so they will let you know the next time something goes wrong.
8. Follow through and follow up. Follow through on getting the problem solved as soon as you can. Go to the client's office and meet face to face if appropriate (it usually is). Even if you turn the problem over to someone else in your company, never lose track of it. Make sure the client receives an acceptable solution. Then follow up a little bit later. Let this person know you've been thinking about the situation and that you want to make sure everything is *really* okay. Give clients permission to complain again; they may have a little more that they need to get off their chests. Remember: *You* are your company's client service department!

Deliver Bad News Right Away

If something is going wrong with a client's order/job/project in a way that will affect the service you ultimately render, let the client know quickly. First, your client may need to protect his or her other business relationships. Second, your client may be able to help you with scheduling adjustments.

Don't just go to clients with a plea for more time or other things that you need *them* to do. Before you call them with a potential problem, think through a few alternatives. Let them know that you are not just asking them to make accommodations; you're working hard on your end as well.

Take Their Satisfaction Temperature

Now that you know the value of the complaining client—that you need to provide opportunities for complaints—and you have the tools to receive the complaints, I suggest you make a habit of taking your clients' *satisfaction temperature* on a regular basis. The nature of your business will determine how often that is for you (annually, semiannually, quarterly, monthly).

When I was selling printing and electronic prepress services, I would take my clients' satisfaction temperature about every 6 months. I tried to do it in person. I'd start by saying something like, "Barbara, I have an important question to ask you. It's important for me to be clear on how well we are serving you. On a scale of 1 to 10, with 1 being miserable and 10 being terrific, how are we doing?"

If I got a 7 or below, I knew I had some unexpressed complaints that needed to be addressed. If I got an 8 or 9, I wanted to see what it would take, in their eyes, for us to do even better.

Another question I've been asking lately is, "What one thing can you think of that could have made this experience better?" Whenever I ask for a satisfaction temperature, I always get great stuff to help me do a better job with all my clients, and I know my clients appreciate my genuine concern for their "business happiness."

The Chinese word for crisis is composed of two picture-characters. One means danger and the other means opportunity. Every complaint and every problem is a "jackpot." One dictionary defines jackpot as "winning when the stakes are high." Don't miss these opportunities to set yourself apart from your competition. If you want to build your business on referrals and word-of-mouth, jackpots are the most difficult and yet the most powerful place to start.

PART THREE

THE SECOND SKILL: PROSPECT FOR REFERRALS

If you're in sales or marketing, you know that the only way to influence people is to demonstrate what's in it for them. Well, what's in it for them to give you referrals? I see two main motives: First, your referral sources have an opportunity to be real heroes to their friends, family members, colleagues, and even their own clients. If working with you truly has been a pleasure, they can look good by helping others learn about you. When you ask referral alliances for referrals, you may be giving them another opportunity to serve one of their prospects or clients. Your alliances may want to call the clients or prospects first, not only to clear the way for the referrals (great for you), but also to make other helping contacts (good for them). Gloria Gault Geary, a successful professional speaker, says, "I bring up my request for referrals as a service to my clients. I give them the opportunity to help their friends and colleagues by telling them about me. It works!"

The second reason for clients to give you referrals is that they want to help you. Don't ever discount the power of this. If you have been serving them well, most clients will derive great pleasure from helping you become more successful. You only have to ask!

Chapter 9

Plant Referral Seeds

"Great movies use foreshadowing. So do great salespeople."

Before attending your referral workshop, I had considered myself highly referable and got used to receiving referrals without asking for them. But I always had the feeling that I was letting great prospects fall through the cracks because I was getting lazy. I used your line with a long-time client of mine. I told her toward the end of our conversation that I was still actively in business and will accept new clients, and that I would appreciate it if she would not keep me a secret. She immediately thought of her sister, who in the past told her she was happy with her financial advisor. This time must have been different. She called me a half hour later at 6:00 p.m. on Friday to tell me her sister would like to discuss with me what to do with one million dollars. I met the sister at 10:30 a.m. the following Monday, and she invested the one million dollars with me. This was the fastest turnaround from prospect to client I have ever experienced. It certainly pays to say "Don't keep me a secret"—not to mention work a little late on Fridays. Thank you for your powerful referral system.

LARRY DENOIA, CPA, CFP
WESTCHESTER, NY

A CLIENT-CENTERED APPROACH

If you've been exposed to any referral strategies in the past, there's a strong chance you were introduced to what I've labeled a "producer-centered" approach to referrals. Many insurance agents have been taught to tell their clients that they get paid in two ways: 1) through commission on a sale, and 2) through referrals. Many salespeople have been taught language such as, "I'm trying to build my business and I need your help."

There is nothing inherently wrong with a producer-centered approach to referrals. In fact, I used to teach a producer-centered methodology. There is, however, a more effective approach. A "client-centered" approach has little to do with you building your business, and everything to do with the value you provide to your clients and their willingness to bring that value to others. It's about your clients helping other people through the products and/or services you sell.

A client-centered approach will bring you three things: First, you're likely to feel more comfortable using a client-centered approach, so you'll actually use it. Second, your clients will feel more comfortable with your request, so you'll get more participation. And third, you'll get better connections to your new prospects. When clients identify one or more people they want to help through the work you do, they will become more involved in making sure you get connected to their friends or colleagues. With a client-centered approach, you'll get more referrals and better connections to your new prospects. Of course, better connections to prospects will yield more new clients, and if you wish to call consumers in their homes, you must get connected (introduced) in some way or you risk being in violation of the do-not-call regulations.

PROMOTE THE REFERRAL PROCESS: PLANT REFERRAL SEEDS

Promoting the referral process by planting referral seeds does three things:

1. It places the notion of giving you referrals (sharing your value with others) into a prospect's or client's unconscious, which makes your future request for referrals easier and softer because it is expected.
2. Planting referral seeds leads to unsolicited referrals from clients down the road.
3. It can often lead to referrals right on the spot by identifying people who are very willing to play the referral game quickly in the relationship. I'll give you a couple of great examples of this in a minute.

FORESHADOW YOUR REQUEST

Screenwriters and directors employ the device of foreshadowing in almost every movie you see. Some seemingly insignificant event happens early in the movie that ties into a very significant event later. This foreshadowing of an event is used for two main purposes: First, it sets up expectations—and the movie had better deliver. (Anton Chekhov, the master playwright, said, "If you show the audience a gun in Act One, someone had better fire it by Act Three.") Second, foreshadowing can help make something that happens more believable. The better the screenwriter and director are at employing this device, the less likely you will consciously notice the foreshadowing.

In the sales process, we can use foreshadowing to set up expectations for some future event. We let our prospects and clients know that, at some point, we may ask them for referrals. Then when we are ready to ask, it's easier for us to do so, and it's easier for them to hear our request. This technique can be applied to other aspects of the sale as well. If there is any part of the selling process that makes you uncomfortable, you can help yourself with foreshadowing.

I was working with a residential remodeling company, teaching architects some selling skills. These architects were required to guide their prospects through a series of small commitments that would eventually result in the sale, and they were having difficulty moving the process along. I suggested that the first time they meet with a prospect, they spell out the entire process: "First, if you like what we discuss this evening, I will ask you for permission to work up some preliminary drawings for the addition to your home. Our fee for that is $500. If you like what you see, the next step is to move into the more complete set of plans. Our fee for that is. . . ." And so on. By telling the prospect exactly what was to come, the architects could much more easily bring up the subject of increasing the commitment. All they had to say was, "Do you remember what I told you our next step would be…? (To draw up the more complete set of plans?) That's right. Well, now it's that time. Shall we go for it?"

Small business owner Lynne Schwabe sows seeds to grow her business all the time. She told me, "We always make it clear from the beginning of a relationship with a client that we build our business by referrals, and therefore client service and high-quality performance are very important to us."

I'll bet you've had a few prospects volunteer referrals to you without your even asking. It's great, isn't it? Now, by planting seeds, you'll discover what being a little more proactive can do for your business.

You can even plant seeds in your written correspondence and promotional literature as well: "94 percent of Bill's clients are obtained through referrals, because they like his work and trust him enough to recommend him to their friends and colleagues." I just met a sales coach named Ramon, who has "By Referral Only" printed on his business cards. I think this is a great idea.

If all you add to your selling toolbox is this seed-planting technique, I guarantee that you will receive more referrals from prospects and clients. This one simple technique can contribute to a significant increase in your sales.

Seven Ways to Plant Referral Seeds

1. With new prospects that you meet through referrals, acknowledge the importance and benefits of the referral process. "Ruth and Joe, my guess is you feel more comfortable sitting down with me today because Grace and Steve recommended my services to you. True?"
2. Say to your clients and prospects, "Don't keep me a secret." "George, I'm glad you see the value of the work I do. Please don't keep this important work a secret."
3. Tell your prospects and new clients, "I want to *earn the right* to know who you know, and I hope to do that by giving you great advice, great implementation, and great service."
4. Tell your prospects and clients, "I'm never too busy to see if I can help any of your friends, family members, or colleagues."
5. Give your clients your business card to carry—as a benefit to them (write their account number on your card and it becomes an important document).
6. Let them know that referrals are a natural outcome of your process. As you sit down with a client to begin your process, say, "Quite often, as I go through this process with others, they begin to think of people who should know about the work I do, but they're often not sure how to introduce me to them. If that comes up for you, please let me know and we can discuss the best way for you to introduce me to them. Make sense?"
7. Share your vision for your business with your clients. When you have a good relationship with a client, say, "I'm building a business based on providing so much value to my clients, they naturally want to tell others about me. Make sense?"

Chapter 10

Ask for Referrals at the Right Time

"You must ask for referrals at the right time, and not a minute before."

I was visiting a client's office and near the end of the appointment I asked him a value-seeking question. He said, "Susan, you know I think you're great. That reminds me. There are three people here who want to talk to you about what you can do for them. Do you have a minute?" I just asked the value-seeking question, and he went right to the referrals. Two of those referrals became clients within a few weeks.

SUSAN NORWOOD
DETROIT, MI

You can ask for referrals from anyone—a prospect, a client, or a referral alliance—anytime you've served them. Notice I said *served* them, not *sold* them. Delivering value is what counts. Of course, they must recognize that you have given them value. Sometimes they'll come right out and tell you they're pleased. Sometimes you have to ask.

IT'S BASED ON YOUR VALUE

My simple formula for knowing when to ask for referrals is "when value has been given and value has been recognized." Pay attention to all the ways your clients tell you that they have seen the value in the work you do. They say things like, "Thank you," "Thanks for fixing the problem," "I didn't know that," "Why didn't my last guy tell me that?" and "I should have done this 20 years ago." These are value-recognizing statements. When you hear these things from your clients—which I assume you do—how do you respond? Do you say, "You're welcome," and then change the subject? Or do you linger a little longer and turn this into an opportunity to plant a referral seed or even ask for referrals?

When a client expresses value recognized, at a minimum you should acknowledge that by saying something like, "I'm glad you're seeing the value in the work we do. You know, I'm never too busy to see if I can help your friends and family members through my work. I hope you won't keep me a secret." This simple little statement can bring you a ton of referrals.

I'd like to see you get in the habit of asking value-seeking questions. At the end of every meeting with a prospect or client, you want to check in to make sure the meeting was helpful or valuable. Don't be afraid of hearing anything negative here. In 95 percent of the cases (as long as you do good work for people), they will have only positive things to say. In the 5 percent chance that they're not happy with something, you need to know about that, and you need to fix the problem.

By the way, when a client has made the decision to buy from you, it's a huge expression of "value recognition." You should always

ask for referrals when someone has made the decision to purchase from you. Of course, you can ask again when you've delivered your product or service.

If you want to truly leverage the lifetime value of your clients, you must continue to stay in contact with them, continue to provide value in any way you can, and continue to ask them for referrals. If they are very open to the referral process you can ask them a few times per year. If they are not as open to the process, ask them once a year (unless they tell you to never ask them again).

WHAT DOES IT TAKE TO PROVIDE VALUE?

Most people have the hardest time asking for referrals from prospects—people they feel they have not yet served. That's why it's so important to find ways to serve your prospects as soon as you can—even in ways that have nothing to do with what you sell. For instance, I know a printing salesperson named Marty who called on a high-quality prospect. This prospect liked Marty and seemed inclined to do business with him. But at the moment she was in need of a printer who could print a special type of label that Marty's company could not produce. Marty, however, found a printer who could serve his prospect, and she was very grateful. Because Marty had planted the seed that he worked from referrals (and accented that concept by referring someone to her), she called him with three hot referrals, and she eventually became a client as well.

Suppose you sell financial services. Can you serve your prospects before you ever sell them? Of course you can. If you structure it carefully, your first appointment with prospects should help them gain so much perspective on their financial situation that they feel you have served them even before they give you any business.

If you sell life insurance, use some type of fact finder to accumulate information that puts you in a position to offer the best products, and serve your prospects by getting them to take a comprehensive look at an area they may not have considered. Serving them this way will help you in two ways: First, your prospects will begin to like and trust you more, and, therefore, will become more likely to buy from you. Second, they will want to share the value you have brought to them with their friends, family members, and colleagues.

If you sell copiers, educate your prospects by bringing them up to date on the latest copier technology. They will feel served before they are sold.

My friend Dave has built a highly successful roofing business. He likes to establish trust by educating his prospects so that they can make the best decisions. He knows they can get a great job from other roofers, but after he educates them without pressure, they tend to sign on with him.

Another way to serve your prospects is to ask what I call high-gain questions. These are questions that probe a little and get your prospects thinking about their situation in ways they may not have previously considered. You can ask them to evaluate, compare, or speculate. If you ask a prospect a question and she says, "Well, I've never thought of that before," then you know you've asked a high-gain question. You serve prospects when you get them thinking.

THE THREE KEYS TO ASKING PROSPECTS FOR REFERRALS

The three keys to asking prospects for referrals are:

1. Serve them before you sell them.
2. Plant seeds that you are building your business from referrals.
3. When the rapport is good, ask them directly for referrals.

In an article entitled "Is Your Networking?" sales trainer Dennis Fox writes, "Not every sale is finalized during the first or second appointment. In fact, many times the sales process is a long-term one, taking months or even years to be consummated. Certainly during that time you have many opportunities to gain the confidence, trust, and

respect of your prospect in order to ask for a referral. Not only that, a completed sale to a referred client can strengthen the resolve of the potential buyer who referred you in the first place."

Kim, a salesperson in Baltimore, pursued a prospect for several months. Most of her prospecting activity with him was spent playing phone tag. When she finally reached the prospect, she learned that he and his company were moving out of state. This move excluded them from doing business together, but during the conversation, rapport was high, so Kim became proactive and asked for a referral. She received three referrals, and two became clients within a month.

The rapport must be right for you to ask people for referrals. They must like you and trust you before they will entertain such a request.

BE FLEXIBLE

One parameter of communication style is "open" versus "guarded." Open people talk about their feelings and let others talk about feelings. They let people into their lives easily. You may call a prospect for the first time, hoping for 5 minutes of her time. The next thing you know you've been on the phone for 20 minutes. You know where her kids go to school, why she's mad at her boss today, and much more. Ask an open person a closed-ended question, and you'll still get an open-ended answer. Open people are usually much easier to gain an appointment with than guarded people.

Guarded people reveal information only when it serves a specific purpose. They operate on a need-to-know basis and are usually uncomfortable sharing their feelings. They let new people into their lives slowly and only on their terms. Ask a guarded person an open-ended question and you'll get a closed-ended answer. ("What types of printing do you buy?" "All kinds.") Unless a guarded person has an explicit need for what you sell and is in a buying mode, it usually takes several contacts to gain an appointment.

What does this have to do with asking for referrals? As you might surmise, open people will feel much more comfortable much sooner with a request for referrals than guarded folks. The more guarded your prospect or client, the more you need to wait for substantial rapport and trust to develop. I've made the mistake of asking guarded people for referrals too soon, and it was painfully clear they were not ready. This doesn't mean you should never ask them for referrals. It just means you must take a little more time and care in building the relationship.

TARGET NICHE MARKETS

Later in this book we'll discuss the benefits and techniques of targeting niche markets. When you target an industry, you gain a great deal of knowledge of that industry and how your various clients handle different challenges. When you call on prospects in your target industry, your knowledge and experience can bring much more value to them. You can discuss issues they are facing with which another salesperson would not be familiar. You can bring them ideas and perspectives that serve them even before you sell them. Targeting niche markets sets up opportunities for you to deliver value right away—even before you complete a sale.

THE GOAL IS STILL MAKING THE SALE

In all this discussion about service, I don't mean to diminish the importance of making the sale. That's still paramount, but when you serve your prospects from the very beginning, the sale becomes much easier. The better you serve clients, referral alliances, and prospects, the higher the quality of referrals you will get. They will take a stake in your success by giving you a steady supply of referrals.

Opportunities to Deliver Value and Become Referable

- When you teach your prospect or client something
- When you get your prospect or client thinking in new ways
- When you (politely) question your prospect's or client's assumptions
- When you do something for them without compensation to you or your company
- When you solve or prevent a problem
- When a prospect makes the decision to become a client
- When a prospect writes you a check to begin the relationship ("happy time")
- When you begin to deliver your product or service
- When you follow up with the delivery of your product or service
- Throughout the lifetime of your client relationships

Chapter 11

Ask for Referrals in an Effective Way

"Ask questions whose answers end with a person's name."

PHIL SIMONIDES

Your referral system has had a huge impact on my sales. I'm getting more referrals than I can handle—a good problem! The other day, using one of your strategies, I asked a prospect for referrals and she gave me a list of 22 great contacts. I've just started calling them, and 3 have already become clients. This system really works!

HARRY SCHIAVONE, JR.
WASHINGTON, DC

There are many ways to ask for referrals. After 10 years of teaching salespeople and small business owners how to ask for referrals, I've crafted a 4-step process that is extremely effective. Thousands of salespeople and small business owners are using this simple approach and achieving great results. As I share this method with you, I'll give you some examples of the words you might use when applying these strategies. I expect you to find your own words—words that are most genuine to you. Use your own words, but make sure you follow the four steps. Leave a step out and you will be less effective.

THE 4-STEP METHOD FOR ASKING FOR REFERRALS™

Step 1: Discuss the Value Recognized

As I mentioned in the previous chapter, you want to hold a "value discussion" at the end of virtually every meeting with a prospect or client. Notice I say "discussion." This is an open-ended conversation. Your job is to ask questions and contribute to the conversation. You want your prospect or client to tell you what value they have seen so far in the meeting, your process, your service, or your product.

When I teach my system to salespeople and small business owners, the mistake I often see is that they use this step as a "value telling." They *tell* the prospect or client what value they've received instead of *asking*. The more you get your prospects and clients to articulate the value they see, the more clear they become about the value.

Again, this is a "discussion," not a "setup." What you *don't* say is, "Have you seen value in the work we've done so far?" ("Yes") "Great, who do you know?" That's a setup that most prospects and clients will not appreciate.

Step 2: Treat the Request with Importance

You must not ask for referrals in an apologetic manner. You must be fully present and confident in your request. The more confident you are in this process, the more confident your clients will be as well.

There are three basic ways you treat your request for referral with importance:

1. Make sure you have enough time. Always use an agenda for your meetings with prospects and clients. *Always!* The last item on your agenda should read "value discussion." This is your reminder (and accountability) to have this discussion. Even if you decide not to go to the next step and ask for referrals, you've still enhanced the relationship with the value discussion.
2. If you met clients through referrals, remind them of that.
3. Transition from the value discussion to your request for referrals with the statement "I have an important question to ask you." How you put it out will determine how it comes back to you. If you put it out in a weak or apologetic way, your clients will not treat you seriously. If you put it out with confidence, they will pay attention, and as a result, you're much more likely to get referrals. Your ability to say, "I have an important question to ask you" will be a true test of your belief in your product or service.

Step 3: Get Permission to Brainstorm (About Bringing the Value to Others)

There are two critical elements to this step: First is the permission step. It's not like we're begging for permission to talk referrals. What we're doing here is getting "buy in" from our prospects or clients. We've found that the politeness of this step actually reduces resistance and increases results. We don't want to make our clients feel uncomfortable. If we just plow ahead and try to get referrals from people who might not feel comfortable giving them, we run the risk of aggravating them. We also give them a clear-cut opportunity to say, "No, I don't like to give referrals." In a future chapter, I'll teach you how to deal with such a statement, but for now, we need to give these people a chance to say no. We don't want to kill these relationships just for a few referrals. Truth is, you can ask for referrals from clients and not get any on the spot, but you can still receive plenty of referrals later from these clients. Some people like to play this game on their terms, not yours. You don't want to alienate them to the process.

The second element in this step is "brainstorming." When I say that word, what other words come to mind? Collaboration? Thinking? Working together? Not judging an idea too quickly? Free-form thinking? That's exactly what we want. We don't want just to ask for referrals and then shut up. We want to participate in the process. When our clients give us permission to brainstorm with them, we can make suggestions. We can qualify who they think about. We have so much more freedom to make sure we get the results we want.

Step 4: Suggest Names and Categories

Here's where you actually brainstorm. If you can, it's always best to begin by suggesting a specific person. If you know your client has a colleague in the business, start there; or a family member, or friend. Whatever fits the situation. Once you've exhausted the individuals you know—or if you don't know any—you move to suggesting categories of people. These categories will vary depending upon your business. I work with a large number of financial advisors, so I'll use their world as an example. The categories a financial advisor might explore are: family, friends, colleagues, and people with "money in motion." They might also ask what I call "trigger questions" to help discover people they can help: "Who do you know who's recently been married?" "Who do you know who's recently had a child, or is about to have a child?" "Who do you know who has recently bought a new home?"

Use Trigger Questions

Every industry has these types of "trigger questions." For instance, I recently trained some folks in the window replacement business. Their trigger questions were: "Who have you discussed this work with?" "Who among your immediate neighbors may also need new

windows?" "Who do you know who lives in an older home who should at least consider replacement windows?"

What are the trigger questions for your industry? One of my clients, Phil Simonides, is a field vice president with American Express Financial Advisors. At one time, Phil was a very successful advisor. Now he trains advisors. Phil, like me, is a real student of the referral game. He says that when you ask for referrals, "You want to ask questions whose answers end with a person's name." This is a great way to think of this step, and even if your prospect or client doesn't know anyone in that category, because you've gotten permission to "brainstorm," you're free to suggest a place to explore.

SAMPLE SCRIPT

I think it's time for an example that illustrates the 4-Step Method for Asking for Referrals™. I'll use a case from the world of financial advisors. You can easily interpret this for your world. Again, don't worry about the words I use. You will find you own words. Just make sure you touch all four bases.

YOU: George, we've been through a process over the last couple of weeks. I've asked you a lot of questions, and you've been very forthcoming with the answers. Now we have a financial plan from which to work. Before we discuss further implementation of this plan, I'd like to reflect on our process up to this point. Please tell me what you've found valuable about this process.

GEORGE: More than anything, I like having very specific goals and a plan to make sure I reach them. I also like the time you took to really get to know me and what's important to me about money, my family, and life in general.

YOU: I know that when we first met you were very concerned about funding your retirement, and also about having enough money for your children's education. With this plan, we'll be starting a 529 program for their education. Do you feel better about these issues now?

GEORGE: Absolutely. Now, of course, I have to make sure I fully implement our plan.

YOU: Well, I'll be working with you to make sure that happens. Anything else that you found valuable?

GEORGE: Well, I really liked your teaching style. You've taught me a lot about how this game works. Plus, I appreciate the courage it took for you to question some of my assumptions about my financial future. I need that from you.

YOU: I appreciate you saying that, and I'm glad you're seeing the value of our work so far. With that in mind, I have an important question to ask you.

GEORGE: Okay, shoot.

YOU: I'm hoping we can brainstorm for a few minutes to see if we can identify some people you care about who should at least know about the work I do and the process I put people through.

GEORGE: Sure, I guess we can try that.

YOU: Great. We're just brainstorming here. There are several places we can explore. Let's begin with your family. I know you have a sister in the area who

has recently been divorced. I suspect this process might be very helpful to her. Would you feel comfortable introducing me to her?

GEORGE: Yes, I would. You're right. She should know about your work. I don't know if she's working with anyone or not.

YOU: Well, maybe she is and maybe not. I'm just looking for an introduction. We'll see where it leads. I'd like to learn more about Linda's situation. But first, let's continue brainstorming a bit more. I have some categories of people to whom I can usually bring great service. Why don't I throw out the categories to you, and you tell me who comes to mind. Okay?

GEORGE: Fine with me.

YOU: You came to me because you were changing jobs and you thought you needed help with your 401(k). Who else do you know is changing jobs?

GEORGE: Well, actually there were five other people in my office who were downsized. You might be able to help them.

YOU: I suspect I might. What are their names?

Notice in the above example when George said he would introduce me to his sister, I didn't immediately start learning more about her. I *do* want to learn about her, but I want to keep the brainstorm alive a little longer. You will get more referrals per session if you keep the brainstorming going for awhile first—then go back to learning more about your new prospects.

If you are targeting a niche market, you might consider pulling out a list of your client's colleagues. You can tell your client you are thinking about calling on them. Ask if you can use his or her name as a reference. Then you can upgrade this "reference" into a real introduction to some of these folks. I call this technique using a "hit list" or "target list." It can be very effective.

USE WORDS THAT ARE NATURAL AND GENUINE FOR YOU

During my many training sessions, some people tell me that they are uncomfortable with the word "brainstorm." They just can't seem to use it naturally. That's fine. Use the word "explore" or the phrases "think about" or "put our heads together." As long as you set it up as a give-and-take situation, you'll be fine.

Variations on Exploring

1. After you gain permission to explore or brainstorm, but before you actually do it, you can put your source more at ease with the referral process by explaining how you will go about contacting anyone who is referred to you. Assure her that if her friend or colleague has no interest in what you are selling, you'll back off immediately. This will show her that your approach will be soft and professional.
2. To ease the tension you may feel in this asking process, you can interject some fun by asking for 100 names. You'll both chuckle for a second. Then when you ask for three names, your request will seem small by comparison, yet it will yield more than just one name.

Chapter 12

Explore Client Resistance

"Don't just try to overcome client resistance. Try to understand it."

Bill, since referral boot camp, I have been averaging one new referral client a week. For my industry, this is quite good. Two things your system helped me realize. First, while I expect clients to give me referrals, I know that they may not. So, I'm not too attached to the outcome. I just ask. This makes me feel less tense, and I think my clients pick up on that. Second, I've discovered that the more confident I am when I ask, the better response I get from my clients. For most of my clients, it's natural for them to want to help bring other people to our process. Thanks again for a great program and great mindset.

Jason Betz
Wilmington, DE

If you work hard to be highly referable, and if you follow the method for asking for referrals that I've provided, the obstacles you encounter when asking for referrals will be minimal. On occasion, however, you may encounter clients who don't feel comfortable with the referral process.

"I don't give referrals."

"I'm not ready to talk referrals yet."

"Let me think about it and get back to you."

"Give me some of your cards to pass out."

Do any of these objections sound familiar? If you've never heard these objections, then clearly you're not asking for referrals often enough.

In my extensive training and speaking on the subject of referrals, I've found that for most sales professionals and small business owners dealing with referral objections is the most difficult part of the referral process. Most people don't know what to do when a client objects to a request for referrals. Most people freeze and bail out too quickly. If this happens enough—sadly—they stop asking altogether. The goal is to hang in there just a bit to explore the objection and see if there's a way to reframe the client's perspective—without jeopardizing the relationship.

THE OBJECTION FORMULA

First I'll give you the formula. Then I'll give you an example of how to apply the formula. (I'll be using an example based on the world of a financial advisor. You can adapt this to your world.)

Step 1: Validate Their Position

Whatever they say, it's okay. Let them know it. You've heard it before. Don't follow the validation with the word "but." This erases your validation. Instead, try transitioning with the word "and."

Step 2: Explore the Nature of Their Resistance

You want to continue this conversation carefully. Explore your client's perspective. Ask a few questions and then try to figure out the objection behind the objection. The initial objection is usually an intellectual response such as "I don't give referrals," but the real objection is usually an emotional response that says "I had a bad experience in the past and I don't ever want that to happen again."

Step 3: Reframe Their Perspective

Once you understand your clients' concerns about giving referrals, you will be able to suggest a way for them to reframe their thinking. *Do not* move on to this step until you have explored their objection first. If you just try to rebut their thinking without fully understanding their perspective, you won't make any progress. In fact, you're more likely to further irritate your client.

Step 4: Collect Referrals

If you've been able to reframe their thinking (an example is just ahead), you can move onto the fourth step in the referral gathering conversation: "Suggest Names and Categories." Begin with a specific person or suggest a category with which to begin.

Step 5: Plant a Seed and Back Off

If your client just doesn't want have this referral conversation, you should respect that, back off, and live to ask another day. Quite often you may ask for referrals, not get any, and 3 months later get a referral from that same client. Therefore you always need to ask.

When you do back off, plant a seed at the end. "Bob, that's fine. We don't have to talk about introductions right now. One simple request: If you run into anyone whom you think might get value from the work I do, don't keep me a secret. Fair enough?"

My rule of thumb is this: If you encounter some resistance, do your best to explore the nature of that resistance and reframe your client's thinking. If your client repeats the objection, gives you a new objection, or communicates through body language changes in a closed-down way, it's time to back off.

SAMPLE CONVERSATION: "I DON'T GIVE REFERRALS"

Here's a typical objection and a possible conversation using the above formula:

YOU: I was hoping we could brainstorm for a couple of minutes about who you care about who might also find value in the work I do. This is the same type of conversation I had with George when he thought of you. Could we do that for a minute?

BOB: Well… actually… I don't give referrals.

YOU: Oh, that's fine. Some folks don't like to give referrals. Can I ask you a quick question about that?

BOB: Well, I guess so.

YOU: When other clients have told me they don't like to give referrals, it seems there are usually two main reasons: Either they've had a bad experience and they don't want anything like that to ever happen again, or they're not sure how their friends or colleagues might react about their names being given out. I'm curious, what's true for you?

BOB: Well, actually, I've had a couple of bad experiences with referrals.

YOU: Sorry to hear that. What happened?

BOB: I gave my best friend's name out to a salesman. This guy bugged my friend for 2 months. My buddy, to this day, won't let me forget it. I've sworn to not give out another referral again.

YOU: I can appreciate your reluctance. I'm wondering if you might indulge me for a second. I'd like to explain how I make contact with the introductions I receive. If you feel comfortable with that, we can go on. If not, no big deal. Okay?

BOB: I guess so.

YOU: Great. I'll probably contact those you'd like to help much the same way I contacted you. I'll have you send them an e-mail to gain permission for me to call them. Then I'll follow up with them with either an e-mail or phone call. In the first conversation with them, I'll see if I can set up a quick meeting. Then we'll take it from there. You may recall we started with a cup of coffee on your way to work one morning. I promise I will do nothing to jeopardize my relationship with you, or your relationships with anyone you know. What do you think?

BOB: Sounds okay, I guess. Let's try one and see how it goes. I do trust you not to embarrass me. If it works, I may have a few others for you.

SAMPLE CONVERSATION—BACKING OFF

Has this ever happened to you? You've served a client well, and he or she recognized the value you delivered. Everything is going great. Then you ask for referrals. Your client doesn't want to talk about referrals. You feel uncomfortable, and so does your client. That's the end of the meeting. Yuk. If that happens a few times, you just might stop asking for referrals.

I've found that knowing how and when to back off from your referral request is about as important as asking in the first place. If you know how to "get out of trouble" with ease, you're more likely to initiate the conversation in the first place.

Most clients really want to tell you the truth about why they don't feel comfortable giving referrals, but most try to "let you down" easy by saying things like "give me some of your business cards" or "let me think about it." We get a "no" disguised as a "maybe." That's why we want to explore the subject from their perspective as best we can. If we fully understand them, they're more likely to open up and listen to a different way to look at it.

As I've said, if a client gives a little resistance, explore it. If the resistance continues (repeating the same objection, giving you a new objection, or changing body language) then it's time to back off. But you don't want to just say, "Okay. Never mind." That won't feel good to you, and it will leave your client a little baffled. You should back off with grace and professionalism. Just as you must ask for referrals with confidence, you must back off from your request (when necessary) with confidence.

We'll pick up our sample conversation at Step 3 of the 4-Step Process for Asking: Permission to Brainstorm. We'll explore the objection. Once we realize our client just doesn't want to participate in the referral conversation, we'll back off.

YOU: I was hoping we could brainstorm for a couple of minutes to see if we can identify some people you care about who should know about my process. Can we try that for a minute?

CLIENT: I don't give referrals.

YOU: I understand. Some folks don't like to give referrals. Can I ask you a quick question about that?

CLIENT: Well, I guess so.

YOU: A few clients have told me they don't like to give referrals. It seems there are usually two main reasons: Either they've had a bad experience and they don't want anything like that to ever happen again, or they're not sure how their friends or colleagues might react to their names being given out. I'm curious, what's true for you?

CLIENT: Well, actually, I've had a couple of bad experiences with referrals.

YOU: Sorry to hear that. What happened?

CLIENT: I gave my best friend's name out to a car salesman. This guy bugged my friend for 2 months. My buddy, to this day, won't let me forget it. I've sworn to not give out another referral again.

YOU: Now I understand your reluctance. I'm wondering if you might indulge me for a second. I'd like to explain how I make contact with the referrals I receive. If you feel comfortable with that, we can go on. If not, no big deal. Okay?

CLIENT: I appreciate your efforts here, but I'm just not comfortable with this."

YOU: I understand. Let me just tell you where I'm coming from and we'll leave it at that. Most people never take the time to do the important work that we've done together. They avoid serious planning with regard to retirement, their children's education, as well as considering the important issues of proper life insurance and disability insurance. So, when in conversation with a friend, family member, or colleague, you determine they should probably know about the work I do, I trust you won't keep me a secret. Make sense?

CLIENT: That's fine. In fact, my son really should be talking to you. He makes a great income, and I suspect he's putting things off. It may take some time, but I'll probably get him to give you a call.

YOU: Sounds great. I'll look forward to it.

Read these sample conversations again with an eye for how I employed the formula. You'll see that I actually validated the client's position. I even gave him a multiple choice of how others feel. In this case I got a referral. If the client didn't want to go there, I would have backed off and planted a seed.

THE THREE THINGS TO REMEMBER

1. Don't try to overcome the objection, just *explore* it to see if there's an objection behind the objection.
2. If the client shows heavy resistance, you should back off and live to ask another day. You don't want to ruin your chances of receiving referrals down the line by pushing too hard.
3. An effective "reframe" is to suggest, "Together, maybe we can craft an approach that you will feel comfortable with."

A decision to not give referrals is usually not a logical one. It's an unconscious emotional decision based on some fear that the client has regarding the referral process. Address those fears and you have a chance to reframe your client's thinking and get referrals.

As you can readily see, the objections that come up in this process need not be intimidating. Your goal is to get comfortable asking for referrals and comfortable when the objections come up. Then, you must be willing to stay with the objection, at least for a little while, to see if it can be turned around.

Chapter 13

The Power of a Profile

"Working with a client that isn't a perfect fit for you and your business is an obligation without commitment."

DAN SULLIVAN

I'm in the top half-percent of my company and have been very successful. Your system has helped me get clearer on who fits my book of business and who doesn't. I'm now focusing on the clients that fit my business perfectly, and not getting bogged down with those that don't. I'm using your referral system to attract only the best clients—and it's working!

DONALD ZARIN
SALT LAKE CITY, UTAH

One way to make sure you receive only the referrals that you want—your ideal clients—is to use an "ideal client profile." This profile is a list of the quantitative and qualitative attributes of your ideal clients. You want to put this profile in writing—on your letterhead. Having it in writing is better than merely speaking it. Our experience has shown that it's more effective when it's put in writing and handed to your potential referral source.

WHO FITS YOUR BUSINESS AND WHO DOESN'T?

First you want to be laser-clear about whom you serve the best and who, in turn, serves your business the best. Not everyone will make a good client for you. Just for a minute, think about your worst clients. What makes them bad clients? What are the quantitative and qualitative attributes of these people or businesses that keep them from being good matches for your business?

Now focus on your best clients. What are the quantitative and qualitative attributes of these people and businesses?

Now which kind of clients do you want more of? Silly question. How do you ensure you attract only "A" clients? How do you ensure that your existing clients and centers of influence refer you to only "A" clients? Simple, you develop your ideal client profile, and you share it with your clients and centers of influence.

Many of the top producers I coach on referrals tell me that the *quantity* of referrals is no longer their pressing issue. Rather, they want to improve the *quality* of the referrals they receive. Have you ever noticed that many clients seem quite comfortable "referring down," but have more difficulty referring "laterally" or "up"? By using an ideal client profile you will solve this problem. Here's how it works.

DETERMINE YOUR "A" CLIENTS

Take a look at your client base and identify your "A" clients. Hint: Your "A" clients are the ones who make you good money (from 50 percent to 80 percent of your revenue over the last couple of years).

Plus, they appreciate what you do for them, you enjoy working with each other, they may be well connected and willing to give referrals, and they are moving your business forward rather than holding you back. Your goal should be to clone these "A" clients. If you can do that, your business will flourish, you'll have more fun, and you'll probably enjoy all the leisure time you want.

Write down the characteristics that define an "A" client—both the quantitative and qualitative. As an example, for a financial advisor, quantitative characteristics are things like occupation, location, age, business, family situation, income, net worth, and assets available for investment. Qualitative characteristics are things like attitude toward professional advice, general personality, a busy schedule, risk tolerance, and so on. Every advisor's profile will be somewhat different. For instance, an advisor might really take pleasure in working with small business owners, while a colleague might enjoy engineers or high-level executives in large companies. There is no right or wrong here. It is simply important to note that when you are working only with people who fit your profile, you do a better job for them, they experience the value you bring to the relationship, and they're more likely to give you referrals to people like themselves.

MAKE IT CLIENT CENTERED

There are two ways you can present your ideal client profile to a client or center of influence: You could say, "Here are the people I'm looking for." This, however, is a *you*-centered approach. Instead, I believe you'll find it more effective to use a *client*-centered approach, such as, "Here are the types of people (or businesses) I've discovered I serve the best." It's a subtle, yet important distinction.

WHAT ABOUT MY "B" CLIENTS?

Of course, you don't forget about your other clients, but you may have a different strategy for maintaining your relationships with them. In most cases, "B" clients have the ability to become "A" clients. You want to work with them in such a way that you help them evolve into "A" clients without taking time away from your current "A" clients. If you have a good relationship with your "Bs," you can still show them your ideal client profile (for "As") without insulting them.

Stop reading for a minute. Get out a piece of paper and start developing your ideal client profile. Even if you never formalize the profile in writing, this exercise will strengthen your ability to explore and brainstorm, and ensure you get the referrals that are best for your business.

Chapter 14

Upgrade the Quality of Your Referrals

"Quantity is great. Quality is even better."

When I first got started in sales, I was focused on activity. I brought on any type of client I could—big or small. Now that I've had some success, I've turned to quality over quantity. I'm using your system as a way to get referred to just the right people.

JEFF HOWARD
TAMPA, FL

Once you have received one or more referrals from your source, your next step is to upgrade the quality of the referrals by learning as much as you can about the prospects. The great thing about referral marketing is that you can learn things about your new prospects from the referral source that you can't learn anywhere else.

What you don't want to do is walk away with just a name and a phone number. When you have a good sense of who you are calling, two things happen: First, the prospect becomes more real to you and you can get excited about making contact with this new prospect. Second, you will be prepared with information about this new prospect that will allow you to have a quality conversation from the very start.

You certainly want to ask some questions that are specific to your industry and your situation. In addition, there are some generic questions that I believe you should ask as well.

QUESTIONS TO UPGRADE YOUR REFERRALS

(Not all of these may apply to your situation, but most will.)

1. Why did you think of her first? Why do you think she's a good match for the work we do?
2. How do you know this person? What is the nature of your relationship?
3. What is his job title or exact position in the company?
4. What can you tell me about her business?
5. What type of personality am I likely to encounter? Is he very direct? Is he very open, or is he more self-contained?
6. Does she have any hobbies or special interests?
7. What are some of the challenges he is facing in general, or might be facing, related to my product/service?
8. Where is the best place to call this person, home or work?
9. When is the best time for me to call to increase my chances of reaching her?

These are the types of things you just can't learn from directories or other lists of prospects (cold research). This warm research can come only from referrals.

WHAT DOES IT TAKE TO GET QUALITY?

The quantity and quality of the information your source gives you will be a combination of three things:

1. Your ability to create enough time during your appointments to have this discussion
2. The relationship you've established with your source: The better the relationship, the more willing your source will be to give you this information
3. Your courage to hang in there in order to upgrade the quality of your referrals

Important: If you've discovered that your prospect has an explicit need for your product or service, you want to ask your source for advice on how to proceed. For example, "How do you think Mary will react to me knowing she's inherited a million dollars? Should I mention it, or should I let it come from her? Your source will coach you on the best course of action here. You want your new prospect to feel comfortable about her name coming up in conversation. Remember: Referral marketing is all about building and protecting relationships. If your referral source advises against bringing it up directly, think of a question that might elicit the information. Example: "I work with people who are concerned with their financial future or who have recently had a change in their financial situation. Might either of those situations be true for you?"

Let's say you obtain a name from your source, and time is running too short to upgrade the referral. No problem! You can call him later that day or the next day and upgrade it some more. I've been given referrals, upgraded them briefly at that time, and then called my source later to gather more information. You might say, "Dave, thanks again for giving me Mary's number. I was about to give her a call and I realized I didn't really know much about her. It would be better for both of us if I could gain a little more information." It's never too late to upgrade the referral.

If you get several names from your referral source, you might ask, "Who should I contact first?" or "If you were me, who would you call first and why?" This will guide your source into the upgrading process smoothly and naturally.

Chapter 15

Get Introduced to Your New Prospect

"Your clients would prefer to be introduced to you by someone they trust. Is this how you're meeting your clients?"

I was with a client a few days after your training session. I used your 4-Step Method for Asking for Referrals. My client's response? "I wondered when you were going to ask me for referrals."

He gave me two. He got one of his friends on the phone with me right in his office and insisted he meet with me. The other prospect called me 2 days later.

MARLA DAVIS
MINNEAPOLIS, MN

I distinguish between three levels of connection you can get when referred to a new prospect. The first level is a *suggestion*. In a suggestion, your referral source plays no role in the contact. You make contact with the referral prospect without any aid from your referral source. The second level is the *introduction*. In the introduction, your referral source contacts the prospect in some way to introduce you. The third, and highest, level is the *face-to-face*. As the name suggests, you are introduced to your new prospect in person. Not all businesses lend themselves to face-to-face introductions. For instance, when your clients are national or even regional in scope, it may be impossible to make a face-to-face introduction. Whenever possible, however, it's the best way to meet a new prospect.

THE SUGGESTION

So you have a name, a phone number, and some information about your new prospect. Your referral source is not providing any introduction or pre-contact on your behalf. While suggestions are not as powerful as introductions, they do have their place—as long as you are making a business-to-business call or the consumer has not registered for the do-not-call list. If you are fairly new with your business, you must create a great deal of activity for yourself—until you reach a critical mass. Suggestions can be a big part of that. Much of my business over the years has started with suggestions.

I usually like to call the prospects I receive through suggestions right away. The most I might do before my initial phone call is send a warm-up e-mail. Otherwise, I'm on the phone, getting the process started.

Some people like to send what's known as a "pre-approach letter," where you send a letter to the prospect before you call. My experience—working with thousands of salespeople—is that pre-approach letters do not lead to more appointments or sales. Although some salespeople feel more comfortable making contact knowing that a letter has preceded their call, I personally think it's a waste of time. Plus, you

have to wait a few days to make sure the letter has been received. Whatever you do, make sure you pick up the phone and call the new prospect without too much delay. I also recommend that, in most cases, you don't send expensive promotional materials to a new prospect without having voice contact with him or her first (or with an assistant). If my prospect is likely to have an assistant, I always go to the assistant first and elicit help in reaching the prospect. Sometimes I'll mail the assistant promotional information if I know he or she will deliver it to the prospect and that I can follow up to secure a phone appointment.

Remember: If you are calling consumers at their homes or on their cell phones, check the do-not-call lists before placing the call (yes, cell phones may be listed on the do-not-call list too).

THE INTRODUCTION

When your referral source introduces you to your new prospect in some way, it's usually much easier to get your calls through and returned. Many prospects will take your calls just out of respect for the referral source (their friend, colleague, or family member).

Plus, if you are calling consumers at home, you can use the introduction as a way to get permission to call your new prospects—even if they are on the do-not-call list.

There are many ways you can be introduced to your new prospect without meeting face to face. Here are a few.

Referral Source Writes a Note on Your Brochure

When you're in the presence of your referral source (you can also do this via mail), have the source write a quick note to the prospect directly on the brochure with a Sharpie or on a sticky note. Now the brochure is personalized for the prospect.

Referral Source Adds a PS to Your Letter

Sometimes I'll have a brief conversation with the source as follows:

ME: Dave, I think what I'll do first before I call Mary is send her a letter letting her know that her name came up in conversation. I'll mention a little about what I do and how I've served you, and then tell her I'll follow up with a phone call. I was hoping I could send you the letter first, along with a pre-addressed stamped envelope. If it looks okay to you, you can send it on. Would that be all right?

DAVE: Yes.

ME: Tell you what: I'll leave space for a PS where you can write a quick personal note to Mary. She might appreciate that. Would that be okay?

I've never had anyone turn me down. Research has shown that the PS is a very powerful part of a letter, and your PS is even more powerful because it's a message from your referral source. Could you ask for a more effective warm-up letter?

Create Special Stationery for Your Referral Source

Here's an idea I got from Hal, my life insurance agent. At our annual lunch, we talked about my needs in his areas of expertise and then we talked referrals. As usual, I had two or three decent referrals for him. Instead of just offering to call these prospects, I waited to see what warm-up method he would choose (if any). He pulled out some stationery he had created with my name on it. It was Monarch-size stationery (6½ by 8½ inches). He had written a sample letter that I could send to these prospects before he called. Although I liked what he had written, I offered to rewrite it in my own words to make it even more personal. I also liked the personal feel of the Monarch stationery. In this case, Hal's new referral prospects received a personal note from me before he contacted them.

Get Your Source to Phone Your New Prospect

I find this tactic to be the most powerful for normal situations. Get the source to call the prospect—not as a favor to you, but to help him protect his relationship with his friend or colleague.

You may have clients who will volunteer to call the prospect right on the spot. If you feel ready to talk to the new prospect (keep it short), then this can work. If you're not ready to talk to the prospect, respectfully decline this idea.

Aside from the benefits this introductory phone call brings to you, there is also something in it for your referral source to make this call, that is, a chance to protect the relationship. Your request might go something like this:

YOU: Dave, I appreciate you giving me Mary's name. I'll call her in a few days. I'm thinking . . . maybe she would prefer hearing from you first so she knows you gave me her name and won't be surprised by my call. Do you think she might appreciate that?

DAVE: That's a good idea, actually. I'll do that.

YOU: Sounds good. Let's see, today is Monday; how about I call her on Thursday? That should give you a couple of days to reach her. Sound reasonable?

(Phrase this request in your own words. Just make it genuine.) Here's another way you could word it:

YOU: Dave, thanks for helping me meet Mary. I was wondering . . . maybe she would appreciate hearing from you first, just to know that you aren't siccing a salesperson on her. Would that be appropriate?

DAVE: Yes, thanks for mentioning that.

YOU: Great. Let's see, this is Monday; I'll probably be able to call her on Thursday. Would that leave you enough time to make a quick call?

DAVE: I think so.

YOU: Thanks. You know, I don't want this to be a hassle for you. If you get her voice mail, a quick message will probably do the trick.

After getting your source's word to call the prospect in the next couple of days, send a fax or e-mail message to the source as soon as you get back to your office, saying something like, "Thanks for the meeting and introducing me to Mary. When you call Mary to let her know I'll be calling, you can assure her that I'll be very professional and will not pressure her in any way." This accomplishes two things: It thanks your referral source (always good to do quickly and often), and it reminds him of the phone call to which he committed.

Now you have your satisfied client or referral alliance saying good things about you behind your back. When you call your prospect, she's expecting your call, she knows why you're calling, and best of all, she's heard good things about you. Could you ask for a better start with a new prospect?

If, for whatever reason, your source will not be calling your new prospect, as you are leaving the appointment you might say, "By the way, when I speak to Mary, I know it's okay to mention your name. If it makes her feel more comfortable, can I suggest that she give you a call as a reference?"

Get Your Source to Send an E-mail to Your New Prospect

E-mail introductions are becoming a popular and an effective alternative to the introductory phone call. There are three great things about being introduced with e-mail: First, it's quite easy for the referral source. It takes little time and effort to write and send the e-mail—much less than to track someone down via phone. Second, you don't

have to wait to hear back from the referral source to see if she had a conversation with her colleague. You can send your own e-mail to the new prospect (not covered by the do-not-call list). Third, you can gain permission from the new prospect to take your call and get his phone number from him (further protection from the do-not-call regulations). When I'm introduced via e-mail, I ask my source to send me a copy. Once I know it's been sent, I wait a day and then send my own e-mail telling the prospect that I plan to call the next day and asking him if he'll be in and if he'll receive my call. I usually end up scheduling a quick phone appointment with the prospect via e-mail as well.

THE FACE-TO-FACE

If your business is geographically limited, you can use the *face-to-face* introduction to full advantage. Of course, the merits of this type of introduction will depend upon your product or service. The less costly your product or service, the more questionable this tactic becomes because of the time and money involved. The more you sell to consumers, the better face-to-face introductions are with regard to the do-not-call regulations. According to the regulations, you may call someone in his home if you 1) have a "relationship" with him, or 2) gain permission to call him. The face-to-face introduction establishes that relationship and allows you to ask for permission.

Get Escorted to His Office or Home

If you sell printing, for example, you may identify another buyer of printing in your client's company, and she can walk you over to his office and introduce you in person. If you sell replacement windows in homes, you might get your clients to walk you over to one of their neighbors who had expressed an interest in the work they were doing to their home.

Take Your Source and Prospect to Lunch

If your referral source and your new prospect are good friends, either professionally or socially, and you get along well with your source, invite the two of them to lunch or dinner (or breakfast—it's cheaper, quicker, and can be accomplished before the work day gets started). You can do this before you actually have an appointment with your new prospect or after the first appointment. Either way, if you can get the two of them together with you, it's pure gold!

Attend Your Source's Association Meeting

If you are targeting a niche industry and you have a client (or a referral alliance) who is somewhat active with the association in that target industry, see if he will take you as a guest to an industry event such as a local monthly meeting. You will then have your satisfied client introducing you, face-to-face, to new prospects.

Treat Your Client and Prospect to a Special Activity

Golfers know that if you pick up their greens fees, they'll follow you anywhere. If you can wrangle tickets to a popular sporting event, you'll make a great connection. Get creative. Invite your client and prospect to the theater, out on your boat (or a rented boat), or to some other fun activity.

Chapter 16

Create a Great Referral Experience

"Giving you a referral should be a pleasurable experience for your clients."

I used your "let's take your friend to lunch together (but I'll pick up the tab)" method. My new client took the referring client out to lunch to say "thanks for introducing us." The results were more business from the first client, new business from the new client, and more trust in me from both of them.

DAN WILLIAMS
CHARLOTTE, NC

I've found that the better the experience your clients have with you in regard to giving you referrals, the more referable you become. Create a great experience for everyone who gives you referrals and you'll stimulate even more referrals.

CONTACT YOUR REFERRAL PROSPECTS RIGHT AWAY

When a client identifies one or more people he would like to help through the work you do, it's important that you make contact with these new prospects as quickly as you can. Whenever I get a referral, I think about my schedule and when I would likely be able to contact the prospect. Then I advise my client of the time frame. In this way, if he is in contact with his colleague before I am, he won't wonder why I haven't yet followed up on his help.

The best policy is to contact your new prospects as soon as you can. Don't let great referrals go stale. If you do, not only will your results diminish, but you'll be burning referral bridges with your clients.

KEEP YOUR REFERRAL SOURCES IN THE LOOP

When people give you referrals, they want and expect you to follow up with them—and they want to *know* that you have. After you've initiated contact with your new prospect, call or send an e-mail to your source to say that the contact has been made. At some point in this process, it's usually a good idea to make voice contact with your referral source to tell about your progress. You'll find that sometimes when you call your source, you'll get other referrals.

There will be times when you'll have trouble reaching your new prospects. Let your clients know. Many of them will step in and help make the connection go through.

Every now and then you may reach a new prospect and the call won't go so well. For instance, the prospect may be annoyed by your call (this won't happen if you've been introduced). If this happens, call your referral sources right away and let them know what happened. Let them know you backed off quickly and that all is okay. It

is better that your referral sources hear from you first. This way, if they hear a minor complaint from their friends, they're not taken by surprise because they already know what has happened.

THANK YOUR REFERRAL SOURCES

After you receive a referral, send your source a thank you note or letter that acknowledges the influence his referral carries, along with a very small gift. I recently obtained five referrals from a client. Mentioning her name opened doors for me. I have already done business with three of the contacts, and the other two still look good. When I called to thank her I said, "You sure are respected out there. All I had to do was mention your name." She was quite flattered.

Right after a client gives you one or more referrals, you also want to send a very small thank you gift. Don't wait for the prospect to become a client. Thank your source for giving the referral. You can send such things as a lottery ticket, a gift coupon to a car wash, or a pass to a movie theater. You can send a sleeve of golf balls, a mug, or a pen with your company's logo on it. Make it easy on yourself. This is not about the money.

Whatever you decide to use as a thank you gift, make sure you keep an inventory on hand. If you have to go shopping each time you get a referral, this technique will quickly break down.

Once that referral turns into a sale, you may choose to send your source a slightly more substantial gift. I like to find gifts that suit my referral source, perhaps something to do with a hobby or special interest. You'll get more bang for your buck if the gift is "thoughtful."

A Word About Paying for Referrals

In most cases, it will not be appropriate to pay a commission to a client who refers you. I believe this cheapens the referral. However, it may be appropriate with some members of your referral alliance to structure a relationship in which you do reward each other for referred business.

Generally speaking, I like to help people with referrals as best I can, knowing it will come back to me at some point.

Marilyn Jennings, the most successful real estate agent in Canada, sends thank you gifts for specific referrals. Twice a year she sends a rather expensive gift basket to everyone with whom she's had a transaction. She encloses a note of thanks for past business and a reminder that she values the person's referrals. She says this one technique alone, although a significant financial commitment, yields tremendous results. She has used it to build a business that's so successful that she has more real estate transactions in a month than the average agent has in a year.

GET THE NEW CLIENT TO THANK THE REFERRAL SOURCE

This simple tactic is so powerful, yet it is rarely used. Once the new prospect has been converted into a new client, get him to thank the referral source. Here are some techniques brought to life with suggested conversations.

1. The Phone Call

YOU: Barb, I'm wondering when you'll be talking to George next?

BARB: I'll be seeing him over the weekend.

YOU: Great. Will you thank him for both of us? He needs to know he did a good thing by putting us together.

BARB: You bet I will.

2. The Card

YOU: Barb, George needs to know he did a good thing by putting us together. I have an idea. I have a card with me that I was going to send to him to say thanks. Why don't we both write a message to him?

BARB: Sounds like a good idea.

YOU: Great. You take this side and I'll take the other. It will look like we're having a party without him.

3. The Lunch

YOU: Barb, I was thinking about taking George to lunch to say thank you for bringing us together. I have a better idea. Why don't we both take him out to lunch? I'll pick up the tab, but the thank you will come from both of us. He needs to know he did a good deed here.

BARB: That works for me. Will I get another lunch if I give you referrals?

YOU: Darn right you will.

4. The Gift

YOU: Barb, George needs to know he did a good thing by bringing us together. Here's what I'd like to do. I have this box of gifts I've put together—lots of little fun things I've found in my travels. Why don't you pick out something you think George will enjoy?

BARB: That sounds like fun. I know he'll love this sleeve of golf balls.

Remember: How you receive your referrals, process the new prospects, and keep your clients in the loop will make a huge difference in your ability to get more referrals from those same clients. Create a "memorable experience" around this process and your clients will enjoy playing the game over and over again.

Chapter 17

Correct Mistaken Assumptions

"Our assumptions drive our behavior. Trouble is, most of the time our assumptions are wrong."

Even though the skills you teach are great, what I really enjoyed about your program was the new referral mindset I've adopted. I used to think that asking for referrals was unprofessional and a sign of not being successful. Your client-centered approach allows me to feel confident and professional while I ask for help in helping others with the work I do.

RICK HURLEY
BETHESDA, MD

NO MORE EXCUSES

Most salespeople don't ask for referrals for several reasons:

1. They don't think about it. It's not part of their mindset.
2. They've never been taught how. They know it's important, but they haven't quite figured out an effective method on their own.
3. They carry with them one or more mistaken assumptions that keep them from being effective with referrals.
4. They are afraid to ask for referrals—for one or more reasons.

Not Part of Their Mindset

In Chapter 3 we discussed what it means to have a referral mindset. In a nutshell, it means that you know the value of the work you do, and you want to leverage that value into introductions to others. With a referral mindset, the referral process is "top of mind awareness" for you. You bring confidence to the process. I hope, if nothing else, this book has given you a strong foundation for a true referral mindset.

Never Been Taught

I can't tell you how many sales reps have come up to me after my referral training to say something like, "My company has always preached the importance of referrals, but they've never shown us how to get them—until now." While this book is not referral *training*, it's the next best thing. I've given you a systematic approach to the referral process that should be easy for you to figure out from here. If not, get your company to contact me and we'll schedule some real training. (Info@ReferralCoach.com)

Mistaken Assumptions

Here is a short list of the most common mistaken assumptions salespeople and small business owners make that keep them from maximizing their referral potential:

- "*I often don't feel I've served my clients enough yet to ask.*" If you ask value-seeking questions at most of your encounters with your clients, you'll always know when you've provided value, and this will become a mute issue.
- "*I don't want my clients to think I'm not successful.*" Many salespeople and small business owners falsely assume that asking for referrals makes them look unsuccessful. They are afraid that they will appear to be "begging" for work. As long as you ask for referrals based on the value you have brought to your clients and your intention of bringing that value to others, you will not look like you are begging. In fact, I believe the more confident you are in the work you do and the problems you solve, the easier it should be for you to ask for referrals. It's the next logical step in the relationship with your clients. You brought them value. Who's the next person to receive it? When you bring most of your clients in from referrals, this whole process gets even easier.
- "*I will look too aggressive and, therefore, hurt the relationship.*" You are not going to hurt your relationships asking for referrals as long as you use the approach I've laid out in this book. You would have to be extremely aggressive and insensitive to hurt your client relationships asking for referrals. I promise you! Use the approach I've given you in this book, and your clients will *never* ask for their checks back when you ask for referrals. I promise!
- "*Most clients feel uncomfortable when asked for referrals.*" No. *Some* clients feel uncomfortable when asked for referrals. Here's the problem: In psychology it's called "projection." We feel or believe a certain thing, and we "project" it onto others. You feel uncomfortable asking for referrals, so you naturally assume others feel uncomfortable being asked. That, however, is not the truth. It's merely your projection. Ask for referrals, and if your client feels uncomfortable, back off. Nothing will be hurt and you'll plant a very powerful seed.

If you're honest with yourself, you'll realize that these mistaken assumptions usually boil down to the fact that you're not comfortable asking, and you've made a decision (usually unconscious) to remain in your comfort zone. Don't let *wimp junction* hold you back from building a highly successful business.

Afraid to Ask

There are many "fears" salespeople encounter with regard to asking for referrals. You might be afraid of jeopardizing the sale, future sales, or the relationship; you might be afraid you're not referable yet (so you don't deserve to ask); or perhaps you're afraid of having your client say, "No, I won't give you referrals." Whatever resistance you might have to asking for referrals, it usually boils down to fear.

Like most fears, this one is a ghost. It appears real, but it's not. If you've done your best to be sincere, if you've served your clients well, and if you've established a relationship of mutual trust, no one will be put off by your request. In fact, they may be extremely happy to help you. Remember to foreshadow your request for referrals by planting referral seeds—then it will be much easier for you to ask.

Doing a good job for your clients, as opposed to just trying to make the sale, builds the confidence necessary to ask for referrals. As I've said, building a business from referrals takes a true attitude of service. Determining when to ask for referrals is partly an intuitive thing. If you don't ask clients for referrals after you know they see the value you bring, just make sure in your heart that it's because the time isn't right, not because you're afraid. Please, please, please don't let fear hold you back from the most powerful way to build your business.

PART FOUR

THE THIRD SKILL: STRATEGIC NETWORKING

The third key strategy, or skill, of this system is strategic networking, that is, forming relationships of mutual support in which each person helps the other build his or her respective business. It's based on the concept that the more you give, the more you get. I call these relationships referral alliances. They are often referred to as *centers of influence*.

I've identified three types of referral alliances: First, there are satisfied clients who, long after you've served them, keep giving you referrals and other connections. Second, there are individuals who may never become clients of yours but who are in a position to give you referrals. And third, there are referral allies who may never be in a position to give you direct referrals but who can help you advance your sales with their advice, wisdom, coaching, and contacts. This section will help you meet and build relationships with all three types of referral alliances.

Chapter 18

Build Your Own Personal Sales Force

*"It's called net-*work, *not net-sit or net-eat."*

Your system made me realize that even though I own a small business and can't afford to hire a salesperson at this time, I can form a "virtual sales force" through networking. I think the most important thing I got from you was "formalizing the relationship" so that all expectations are out on the table. I now have seven powerful people actively looking for new business for me, and I for them.

MARIAH MARTIN
DALLAS, TX

IS NETWORKING DEAD?

Networking is an overused word and an underused strategy among many salespeople and small business owners. It's definitely not dead. These days, when many people think of networking, they think of going to business events in search of business opportunities. But networking is so much more than an event. It's a way of doing business and a way of generating substantial referrals.

Bob Burg, author of *Endless Referrals: Network Your Everyday Contacts into Sales* (McGraw-Hill, 1994) says, "Real networking is the cultivation of mutually beneficial, give and take, win/win relationships." When done correctly and with genuine care for the success of others in your network, this results in an enormous increase in referrals.

I like to use the term *referral alliances* instead of networking because I want to emphasize two important points: First, it's strategic. Your network of contacts becomes a well thought-out part of your overall marketing strategy. Second, it's an alliance. Your network of contacts is not just a bunch of people you know. You work together to bring each other as many win/win opportunities as possible.

Lynne Waymon is one of this country's leading experts on networking. Lynne says, "Networking, in its pure form, enables business people to further their own goals while helping others further theirs. It should be a positive step in the right direction for everyone on the road to success. Networking is a process of building business relationships for the long term."

Bob Burg says networking is "the building, cultivating, and developing of a very large and diverse group of people who will gladly and continually refer you lots and lots of business, while you, in turn, do the same for them." He also says, "All things being equal, people will do business with and refer business to those people who they know, like, and trust."

Dr. Ivan Misner, founder of Business Network International, says, "Networks are coalitions of business professionals who, through

a mutual support system, help each other do more business. It must be based on the concept that givers gain." The mutual support system that he mentions can come from a specific organization that assists people with networking, from networking events, or from what you build with your own initiative and creativity. The point is that you must ally yourself with people who can help you obtain more referrals.

CONTACT SPHERES

Ivan Misner talks about a concept he calls *contact spheres.* Every industry has its own set of contact spheres—salespeople, business owners, and other professionals who can provide you with a steady source of good leads and introductions. They tend to work in areas that complement rather than compete with your business. Misner says, "For example, if you were to put a lawyer, a CPA, a financial planner, and a banker in the same room for an hour, you couldn't stop them from doing business. Each of them has clients that could benefit from services of the others."

Here are some examples of contact spheres:

1. *Financial Services*: Financial planners and advisors, insurance agents, CPAs, estate planning attorneys, human resource directors, association benefits managers, trust officers, and mutual fund wholesalers
2. *Graphic Communication*: Printers, graphic artists, promotional products brokers, marketing consultants, paper salespeople, color separators, and non-competing printers and artists
3. *Real Estate Services*: Residential agents, commercial agents, escrow companies, title companies, mortgage brokers, appraisers, photographers, contractors, plumbers, caterers, gardeners, exterminators, home inspectors, florists, and roofers
4. *Home Contractors*: Painters, carpenters, plumbers, landscapers, electricians, roofers, flooring companies, window

replacement companies, sun room companies, fence companies, and real estate agents

5. *Special Occasion Services*: Photographers, caterers, travel agents, florists, musicians, DJs, bakers, event planners, and tent companies

What is the natural contact sphere for your industry? Who should be on your target list of potential referral alliances?

Kevin Brown is a sales manager for a printer in the Washington, D.C., area. One of his company's services is designing business forms. Kevin has formed referral alliances with other commercial printers. When his printer alliances run across a client or prospect who needs forms, they always refer Kevin. Even though Kevin's company can do some of the other types of printing, these referral alliances trust him not to go after their commercial business.

I was giving a presentation in Richmond, Virginia, and had arranged with an airport transportation service to be driven from the hotel to the airport for my flight home. Boris Marks picked me up and we got to talking. Boris owns a business he calls Designated Driver. He and his drivers are on call to assist people who have had too much to drink and need a ride home. What is unique about Boris's business is that he not only drives the client home, but he drives the client's car home as well.

Boris's business is booming because of his ability to form referral alliances. He has made alliances with bartenders, the ABC board, restaurants, police officers, and others. Each of these groups of alliances serves Boris with referrals, and Boris serves them too by making their jobs easier. How can you make this strategy work for your business?

YOU MAY ALREADY BE USING REFERRAL ALLIANCES

You may have already formed some referral alliances. If so, you know how they can help you gather referrals that turn into sales. The key

questions are: Are you doing it as effectively as you could be? Are you constantly looking for new alliances? Are you investing the time to nurture and deepen the relationships you form so that each party knows exactly what the other does and how they can benefit their respective clients?

Here are some key steps you should take to maximize your relationships with referral alliances:

1. Teach each other about your respective businesses. Answer the following questions for each other: Who are good prospects for your business? How do you serve them? How is your product/service different from your competitors? How would I know good prospects for your business if I ran into them?
2. Bring your business to life with stories, anecdotes, and case studies. It's one thing to list your products and services, but it's another thing to humanize them with real-life situations. Tell each other how you've solved specific client problems.
3. Discuss how you'd like to receive referrals. Don't assume your referral alliances know the best way to refer someone to you. Come to an agreement about it. At minimum, you want to make sure your prospect is expecting your call.
4. Receive the referrals you get in the best way:
   - Make contact with new prospects as soon as you can.
   - Keep referral sources advised of your progress.
   - Thank referral sources with small gifts.
   - If prospects become clients, get the clients to thank the referral sources (this makes the sources heroes, and it makes you more referable).

This all goes beyond networking organizations and networking events. In order to build a business in which you work only from referrals, you must tune your awareness to everyone who comes into your life who might become a referral alliance. Stop and think about the types of people you should be meeting and with whom you should be nurturing referral relationships. Be open to people who at first glance may not look like good prospects. They may become great allies. When your awareness is tuned into forming these types of relationships, more opportunities will present themselves.

A referral from another salesperson can be as powerful as a referral from a satisfied client. Let's say, for example, your referral alliance is in the office of one of his clients, and that client needs something the salesperson can't deliver. If that salesperson knows how you truly benefit your clients, he can recommend you with confidence and enthusiasm. All the goodwill and trust he has established with his client will then be transferred to you. You work off this *borrowed trust* until you begin to establish your own trust.

THE WIN/WIN ALLIANCE

Your alliances should be productive for everyone involved. There are some important things you must do to make sure your referral alliances become productive sources of referrals. First, you must find ways to serve them.

1. Give them referrals.
2. Help them solve problems through your network of contacts.
3. Give them advice.
4. Be a good listener when they need one.
5. Find out what success means to them, and then help them get there.

Second, you must work your network. It's called net-*work*, not net-sit or net-eat. If you want to build a prosperous word-of-mouth business, you must work at it. Find ways to stay in touch with your referral alliances. Merely knowing them is not enough; you must nurture these relationships.

Your referral alliances will give you referrals because:

1. You've served them well, and they want to pay you back.

2. They want to be heroes to their customers, clients, or associates by referring them to other great products and services.
3. They know that helping you will come back to them one way or another.
4. They truly want to contribute to your success because they like and trust you.

I know some salespeople who have built incredible careers through strategic networking. Just as referral marketing is more than a bunch of techniques (it is a way of thinking), so too is this concept of forming referral alliances. You must act on the knowledge that building strong, mutually beneficial relationships with people, even those who may never buy what you sell, will take you to higher levels of success.

Chapter 19

Have a Strategy for Business Events

"Networking is not just an event, it's a long-term strategy."

I went to a networking event 2 days after your seminar. I ran into a long-time client of mine and decided to use one of your strategies. I asked her who a good prospect for her business would be and how I would know it. She opened up to me about her business, which put me in a position to help her through referrals and other means. Then she turned the conversation around to me and who would be a good prospect for my business. Now she's actively looking for opportunities to refer people to me.

BOBBY FURST
CHICAGO, IL

Most salespeople and small business owners don't take full advantage of the business events they attend for two reasons: 1) they are too short-term in their thinking, and 2) they don't know how to work the event in a way that produces results. Here are some solid ideas for getting the most out of your networking efforts at business-networking events.

HAVE A LONG-TERM STRATEGY

In order to make the most of networking it's best to have a long-term strategy. Lynne Waymon, my colleague and networking expert (www.ContactsCount.com), likes to tell the story of a man who said to her, "I tried networking last Thursday. It doesn't work!" For your networking efforts to really produce results, you can't think short-term. First, you need to know who you are looking for. Have you identified, as we covered in the last chapter, the types of people who make great referral alliances for you? Second, do you know how and where you will meet these referral alliances? To what associations or other business groups do they belong? Can you go to their meetings as a guest? Are they groups worth joining? Third, do you know what you want from them and what you're able to offer in return?

Are you able to communicate what you do, how you do it, who you do it for, and how you truly bring value to others in a way that's clear and concise and that generates keen interest?

Who Do You Want to Meet?

Here's the range of people you will find at business-networking events with whom you want to connect:

1. Actual prospects
2. People who work for companies that you want to prospect
3. Alliance candidates who can generate referrals for you
4. Candidates who can help you with business advice, wisdom, and their network

5. Interesting people representing interesting products and services who can become part of your personal catalog of products and services that you can tap into in your effort to help others

GO FROM TALKING TO TRUSTING

Lynne Waymon talks about four stages of networking. The first stage is all too common, yet it's one to avoid. It's called Taking. It involves the "me, me, me" attitude. It means saying, "Hi, I sell specialty advertising products. If you ever need anything, give me a call. Bye now." Like kissing too soon on the first date, it's offensive and rarely leads to good relationships. I sometimes refer to this as "drive-by" networking. You know what I mean. You're at an event talking to a few people and someone abruptly joins the group. He then quickly hands everyone his business card. He says a few things about himself, and then he's on to the next group. Don't *you* do this!

The second stage is called Trading. This is a little more productive. That's when *I* own a tree-cutting service and *you* need to have trees cut down. You find someone who needs what you sell, or vice versa.

The third stage is called Teaching. Networking is a process of teaching people about yourself and your business—and, of course, learning about them and their businesses as well.

According to Waymon, the fourth and highest stage of networking is Trusting. The best networkers build trust by showing their character and competence over the long haul. Where trust has been built, referrals flow freely.

JOIN THE RIGHT ORGANIZATIONS

One basic element to good networking is joining certain key organizations. There are several types of groups you might choose. You can choose a group because of the resources, referrals, and support you can get. You can also choose groups that might actually have prospective clients as members. Some groups might be a combination of the two.

Waymon says, "Choose organizations that have a strong networking culture. When you go to the meetings, do the members seem upbeat, interested, interesting? Are there ways, formal and informal, for people to meet each other? Are newcomers welcomed, and are there ways to become visible? Is the organization growing and thriving, or dying and depressing?"

Of course, joining an organization is not enough. You can pay your dues, read the newsletter, and attend events, and still not have a network. You have to become visible to make your membership worth your time. Contribute your skills, give out name tags, make an announcement, or write a newsletter article. By the way, introduce yourself to the officers. Tell them what you're interested in. Talk to the speaker before each meeting. You may even be mentioned by that speaker. That's visibility.

Rick Hill, a professional speaker and author, suggests that you don't join an organization just to get leads. Join because you want to get involved. If you're there just for leads, you'll probably come on too strong or give up too early (not to mention always be in a "taking" mode). Rick says that if you enjoy the work the association does, you'll get more involved, and better-quality leads will result. These will be stronger referrals and much easier to come by.

I can't emphasize this point enough. If you are going to take the time and expense to join an organization, the best way to get referrals from it is to become active among its members. When I was first getting started as a professional speaker, I made a great decision. I joined the National Speakers Association as well as the local chapter in Washington, D.C. I was there to learn from people who did what I did. I knew it would help me build my business, but I never thought I'd get business directly from the association.

In my second year of membership, our local chapter was led by a hard-working professional named Wolf Rinke. (If you ever need a great speaker, just cry "Wolf.") During Wolf's tenure as president of

our chapter, I worked hard on our first Speaker's University. A month or so after the school was finished, Wolf gave me a call. He had been contacted by Sommers Communications, a company in Atlanta, that had just won a large seminar contract and needed several high-quality speakers. It was not the right match for Wolf, so he wondered if I was interested. He told me that one reason he called me was because I had worked so hard for him. (I served him!) Well, my contract with Sommers Communications resulted in a long-term relationship of well over 150 paid speaking engagements to date. That's significant!

Don't expect to get business from an organization unless you truly involve yourself, become visible, and serve others.

UPGRADE YOUR NETWORKING PARTNERS

All of us have limited time to spend in the networking phase of business development. Lynne Waymon offers these distinctions as a way to determine those with whom you should spend your time. She says, "Think of a bull's eye with concentric circles. On the outside rim are *Acquaintances*, on the next inner ring are the *Associates*, then come the *Actors*, then the *Advocates*, and finally the *Allies*."

- *Acquaintances*: There's no circle around these folks because they barely know who you are. You bump into them from time to time. You're not in their network, and they're not in yours. An acquaintance is usually a non-productive relationship. To create productivity with these people, you must upgrade them to associates.
- *Associates*: You see these people regularly because you have chosen to join a group that brings you in contact with them, or because you are pursuing contact with one another outside of any formal group. Since you are meeting regularly, you have the opportunity to get to know these people in your respective areas of competence. As you begin to know and

appreciate one another, opportunities for referrals and other help begin to emerge. Mutually beneficial exchanges will flourish as you and your contacts become associates.

- *Actors*: Think of actors on a stage. They are in a dialogue. Something's happening between them. Actors are the people in your life with whom you are actively exchanging valuable information and resources. Over time, as trust grows, you become interested in adding to each other's success. When you really tune in to what your contact is looking for, you move him or her from an associate to an actor.
- *Advocates*: Advocates are people who go out of their way to find opportunities to refer and recommend you to others. They are so confident in your abilities and your integrity that they are willing to put their good names on the line to promote you. Advocates make sure the people you want to meet hear about you before they hear from you.
- *Allies*: Think of these people as being your very own board of trustees. They care about your success. They give you advice that you respect because they have become experts on you. They cheer you on in every arena of your life. They give you a nudge when you need it most. They celebrate your successes with as much enthusiasm as you do theirs. You won't have time to cultivate too many relationships at this level, so you must select these people carefully.

Lynne adds, "One word of warning: You'll be labeled a *nuisance networker* if you violate the natural progression of networking contacts. You must allow the trust to develop comfortably for all parties." Use these distinctions to evaluate where you are in relationship with the people in your network. Make a list of all of your significant networking contacts and place them in the categories Lynne outlined above. Then, determine your next action step to upgrade the quality of those contacts.

Chapter 20

Get the Most Out of Business Events

"Be a serve *person first, and a salesperson second."*

To make sure I get the most out of business events, I find a colleague to hold me accountable. I tell him or her my goals for the event. Then I ask him or her to check in with me the next day and give me a hard time if I don't work hard to accomplish the goals. The fear of my colleague calling me a wimp moves me through any fears or awkwardness I encounter at the event itself.

Joel Darling
Portland, OR

PREPARE TO BE SPONTANEOUS

When you're at a business event, you don't want to use a canned approach toward each person you meet. On the other hand, you want to make your conversations count. Be prepared to be spontaneous. *Plan* your answer to the question "How are you?" or "What's new?" Talk about a resource you've found, a client you helped, or some "win" you've just had. Be ready to ask about things you'd like to find, learn, or connect with. When someone says, "What's new?" have your conversation agenda ready—and be natural.

I like to come to events ready to talk about one major win I've just had and one challenge I'm facing. I get out of the "What's new?" dead end by saying, "Let me tell you about a great win I just had, and then you can tell me one." A good conversation will usually develop. Sometimes people thank me for helping them remember the good stuff that's happening in their lives.

HAVE A GOAL FOR BUSINESS EVENTS

I can deliver a speech to any size audience, but in a networking environment, I can be a bit shy with strangers. To combat this, I've turned to setting goals to help me increase my effectiveness. Here are some typical goals I've set going into business events to help me maximize my results:

1. Have significant conversations with at least three new people
2. Meet the speaker, have a good conversation, and see if I can serve her
3. Have a conversation with the association leader and serve her in some way
4. Introduce at least two people to each other

Setting little goals like these usually keeps me from wimping out. The only thing that commits me to the goals is my word to

myself. Do I ever slip? Of course. When I keep my word, do I get good stuff? You bet!

If you are shy at business events, Lynne Waymon suggests you come prepared with a few openers such as, "What brings you to tonight's meeting?" or "This is my first time here. Have you been a member long?" or "I came here hoping to meet other people who have home-based businesses. Is that why you're here?"

Lynne adds one more tip: "Make sure your body language reflects your desire to meet people. All too often I see people standing around with a vaguely bored look on their face, eating another olive. Instead, smile, look confident, and go out of your way to greet people. Just last night I made a wonderful contact by introducing myself to someone in the hotel lobby who was obviously looking for the same meeting I was."

Bob Burg says, "When meeting a networking prospect for the first time, invest 99.9 percent of the conversation in asking questions about that person and their business. They want to talk about their business, not yours—let them. The people who we find most interesting are the people who seem most interested in us."

Sometimes I'll offer to assist with registration for a while. This sets me up as a host. I can see the people who are coming in and meet them, and then it's easier to approach them later on.

IT'S IMPORTANT TO REMEMBER NAMES

It's not surprising that so many people say, "I can never remember names." The next time you're at an event, count the number of seconds people spend in the name exchange. It's less than 5 seconds. The key to remembering someone's name is to linger longer over the name. Ask about the other person's name. "Is that Linda with a *y* or an *i*?" "Do you like to be called William or Bill?" Then be ready to teach them your name. Nothing fancy here, just a tip for remembering. I often say, "That's Cates with a *C* not a *G*." Then we get to laugh about how much money I don't have because my name is Bill Cates instead of Bill Gates (founder and CEO of Microsoft).

WHAT DO YOU DO?

Bob Burg recommends that you have an opening statement prepared that says what you do and how it benefits others. "When someone asks what you do, don't just say, 'I'm in advertising.' Or 'I'm a financial advisor.' Or 'I sell printing.' A better statement would be, 'I help people create long-term wealth and financial security.' Or 'I am a printing consultant. I help people get the best possible printed piece at a competitive price.'"

You get the idea. You can say what you do, and then follow it with a simple benefit statement. I suggest you talk about your job in a way that makes you look different from all the other people who do what you do. Tell them what makes you different. This will help you stand out in their minds so they will remember you, and it might trigger an interesting conversation.

Let me share how I've tried to differentiate myself from the thousands of people who write and talk on the subject of sales and marketing. Sales and marketing speakers are a dime a dozen. Good speakers are a quarter a dozen. It didn't take me long to learn that I had to find a way to separate myself from the crowd, so I decided to become this country's foremost expert in how to build a business through referrals and word of mouth. There are only a handful of sales and marketing experts who have this "referral" focus. This focus helps people see how I'm different from most other sales and marketing experts.

ARE YOU WAITING TO TALK OR WAITING TO LISTEN?

To establish rapport and learn ways to serve others, you have to ask good questions and be a good listener. Most people like talking about themselves and their businesses. Just as you use good questions to probe your prospects on a sales call, do the same with people you

meet at business events. Get them talking. Learn about their challenges as well as their successes. Be a focused, active listener. Gain their trust by serving them first. Even if they aren't candidates for future business, you can still serve them. It's fun to do—and you never know how it might come back to help you.

Good Questions to Ask

In *Endless Referrals*, Bob Burg offers these questions to ask at business events:

1. How did you get started in the widget business?
2. What do you enjoy most about your profession?
3. What separates your company from your competition? (This will allow folks to brag, or it will serve them by getting them to think about this important question. By the way, make sure you have an up-to-date answer.)
4. What advice would you give someone just starting in your industry?
5. What one thing would you do with your business if you knew you could not fail?
6. What significant changes have you seen take place in your profession over the years?
7. What do you see as the coming trend in your business/industry?
8. What is the strangest or funniest experience you've had in your business?
9. What have you found to be the best ways to promote your business?
10. What one sentence would you like people to use in describing the way you do business?

Here's one I like to use: "If I were talking with someone who might be a great prospect for your business, how would I know it, and how would you like me to introduce that person to you?" Very powerful!

You must be in a place in your heart and mind where you truly want people to tell their story and you don't care if you tell your story. You're there to meet people and learn about them so that you can serve them so that they will serve you in return. You must understand that you are not there to tell your story first.

DON'T FIRE-HOSE PEOPLE

Sometimes you meet bona fide prospects at a business event—people with a clear need for what you sell. Naturally, you get excited, but don't do what speaker and author Rick Hill calls *fire-hosing*—dumping information on them. Unless you've established some rapport, this behavior will work against you. Ask some questions and explore their situation. Then, at some point, get their card and permission to follow up. You might try to set up an appointment if the rapport is high, or you could wait until a little later in the event.

Whenever I am getting permission to call someone later, I ask, "When I call, will I get straight to you or am I likely to get your voice mail?" Or, jokingly, "Do you have a well-trained gatekeeper?" Then we discuss how I get past this "barrier." Sometimes, if I haven't qualified people enough to want an appointment, or if I don't have my calendar with me, I'll schedule a phone appointment for the next day. This way the prospect is expecting my call, and I will get past any barriers.

I believe that high-caliber networkers *focus* their efforts. First, target those who will give the greatest return—the leaders and most successful people within the group. Find a way to serve them, at the event itself or later.

Tips for Better Connections

- *Maintain good eye contact.* At business events, good eye contact is important, and maintaining it takes some discipline. It's easy to become distracted by friends or colleagues walking by. When you're talking to a new acquaintance and your eyes are wandering, he or she may get the impression that you're just killing time until someone better comes along.
- *Manage interruptions.* Be careful how you allow interruptions by people who know you well. Be gracious and introduce your old friend to your new acquaintance. If you and your acquaintance are getting into a good conversation, you might say to your friend, "Brian, it's great to see you. I was just learning about Terrie's business. Tell you what, give me a few minutes with her and I'll catch up to you. Okay?"
- *Find a networking buddy.* If meeting people at business events is not always easy for you, find someone to accompany you to the event, but don't use that person as a crutch for your fear. Rather, make an agreement to introduce people to each other and invite each other into conversations. Introduce each other in glowing terms. Help the whole group get excited about meeting the two of you.
- *Meet the speaker.* If the business event you're attending has a guest speaker, meet the speaker and strike up a conversation. Make sure he or she knows what you do and how you benefit others. Then sit up front with your name tag where it is highly visible, and there's a good chance you'll get mentioned in the program. Do this at every meeting and you'll be known by everyone in no time.
- *Don't forget to follow up.* When you meet people at an event with whom you'd like to begin building a relationship, it's a good idea to reconnect with them later in the event if there's time. Look for reasons to reconnect. For instance, you might meet someone else they would enjoy meeting. You might have an idea for them. Demonstrate that you remember their name. Before you leave the event you might say good-bye to the two or three people with whom you want to stay in contact.

Chapter 21

It's Not Over When the Event Is Over

"Those who fail to follow up usually fail."

True story. I went to a Chamber of Commerce event a week after your program for our company. I collected 15 great business cards. In the past, I would usually follow up on a few and toss the rest. This time, I called all 15. The one contact I made that I was certain was a waste of time turned into the best contact of all. While he was not a good match for my business, he gave me 5 great referrals. I've already done business with 3 of them. Amazing! I will never fail to follow up again.

Randy Robertson
Toledo, OH

EVALUATE YOUR SUCCESS

After each business event, take a few minutes to evaluate your success. Ask yourself such questions as:

1. Did I hit my goal for the number of people I wanted to meet? If not, why not?
2. Did I listen actively and generously?
3. With each significant contact, did I find a reason to connect with that person later?
4. Did I get there early to help out or talk to the centers of influence?
5. Do I have time set aside to follow up with people promptly—to do what I said I would do?
6. Did I volunteer in a way that would show off my talents or help me learn new skills?
7. Did I step out of my comfort zone to meet new people and have genuine conversations with them?
8. Did I have an attitude of giving? Was I looking for ways to give first?

FOLLOW UP AFTER THE EVENT

Remember: According to networking expert Lynne Waymon, the highest levels of networking are *teaching* and *trusting*. Find a way to serve people in a genuine way. Help them fix a problem or find an opportunity no matter how small it may seem. After you've served them, they will be much more receptive to being taught about *your* business as well as how they might help you.

Even if the meeting at the event didn't create a specific reason to call back, I try to call, or at least e-mail, all those people with whom I had a significant encounter within a day or two after the event. I either have something specific to say, or I simply clarify who they are and what they do, and make sure they're clear

about me. When appropriate, I try to set up a phone appointment to explore possibilities.

When I meet actual prospects at an event and can think of something appropriate, I send them something non-sales related, something other than my brochure. This will show them that I am interested in more than just selling them something or using them for referrals. I'm interested in a mutually beneficial relationship.

I recently heard of a successful salesperson who has a reputation for sending his clients, prospects, and referral allies vacation photos that he turns into personal postcards. He takes such funny and creative photos that everyone on his list looks forward to his next vacation.

Lynne Waymon says, "One way to assess how you're doing at building a circle of contacts (a network) is to ask yourself once a week, 'Who do I have to thank this week?' Reconnect by thanking people who've contributed in any way at all to your success that week—with support, information, resources, ideas, referrals. Give them a call, send them an email, send flowers, or offer to help them. Find a way to acknowledge their help. What a great way to spend Friday afternoon! If you've got at least five people to thank, give yourself a pat on the back. I truly believe that as our capacity for gratitude grows, our ability to give grows. And givers always make a great connection."

Networking at events is one of the fastest ways to find referral alliances that will help you build your business as you help them build theirs. Remember: Networking is much more than just going to events. It means being *strategic* about whom you want to meet and how you want to stay in contact with them.

The Ten Commandments of Networking

1. Have your networking tools with you at all times: plenty of business cards, brochures, and a pocket-sized business-card file that has the cards of the professionals you prefer.
2. Set a goal for the number of people you want to meet. Some people go to a meeting with only one goal in mind: disappearing at the time they plan to leave! To get the most out of a networking event, don't leave until you've met your quota of people.
3. Act like a host, not a guest. How would you act at any type of business event if *you* were the host? Would you be more outgoing? Would you be in a giving mode? Would you watch for lulls in conversations and introduce people to each other? Act like the host and you'll make more quality contacts, or actually get involved in the organization and host an event.
4. Ask strong probing questions. Don't just stay on the surface with people you meet.
5. Give a lead, a referral, or an idea whenever possible. Go to events to give first.
6. Describe your product or service in a way that shows how you benefit your clients. Bring your business benefits to life with stories, anecdotes, and case studies.
7. Exchange business cards with people you meet. Don't just give them yours. Get theirs and write notes on the back to remind yourself of your conversation. When you get back to your office, you can recall the conversations and take the appropriate action.
8. Spend more time with new contacts and less time with friends and associates. If you meet someone who could be an incredible referral alliance, invest time with them to make sure you form a good connection—and remember to follow up the conversation later.
9. Put time and energy into remembering people's names. Linger a little longer on names when you are being introduced.
10. Follow up with the people you meet. Good follow-up is the lifeblood of networking. You can obey the previous nine commandments religiously, but if you don't follow up effectively, you're wasting your time!

PART FIVE

THE FOURTH SKILL: TARGET NICHE MARKETS

Targeting a narrowly defined market is the fourth and final skill in building a referral-based business. Whether you are a small business owner or a company salesperson, niche marketing will help you substantially increase your income and inject some fun into selling. Let's start with a definition. Targeting niche markets means positioning yourself as an expert in a target industry as it relates to your product or service, and leveraging that expertise and reputation with appropriate marketing techniques. This way, people in the target industry will think of you first. You may already be targeting some industries, or you may have thought about targeting, but you didn't know how to do so effectively. This part will show you how.

Chapter 22

Your Most Powerful Marketing Strategy

"Birds of a feather flock together."

I built a very successful business focusing on a very clear niche. I got a little restless and thought I'd expand out of our niche. What I found is that we weren't nearly as good outside our niche and the business wasn't as profitable, so I recommitted our business to our niche. We even bought another business that focused on our niche. Profits are higher than ever before.

MONICA ROSEN
NEW YORK, NY

What's the difference between marketing and selling? Basically, marketing is all the activity that makes a sale possible. Marketing makes people aware of your product or service and puts them in a position to meet you in the most favorable of circumstances. Bill Brooks, author and speaker, says, "Marketing strategy is what gets you to the client's door in the best possible light. Sales strategy is what you do when you are inside."

THE BENEFITS OF TARGETING NICHE MARKETS

The strategies in this part take the basic principles of positioning and marketing, and make them applicable to any salesperson or small business owner. Not everyone will take the time to put these strategies into action, but those who do will reap the rich rewards of creating a great reputation within a narrowly focused market.

There are at least three compelling reasons for targeting one or more niche markets:

1. Word of mouth is much easier to create. A great reputation with people saying good things about you behind your back is the most effective way to ensure sustained success. Witness a new movie hitting the theaters. If the movie isn't good, word of mouth kills it. If the movie is good, word of mouth turns it into a hit. Word of mouth often has much more impact in the marketplace than the reviews published by movie critics. It's the same with books, audio programs, and virtually anything else anyone tries to market. If the product or service is superior, people start to talk about it. That's what I want for you.
2. Referrals are easier to obtain. People within narrowly defined markets usually have many friends and colleagues to whom they can refer you. When they know you are concentrating your efforts in their industry, they are usually more willing to help you extend your influence. In my own niche marketing efforts, I have rarely met a client who was concerned about me working for the competition. In fact, quite often, competing busi-

nesses are on very friendly terms with each other. I've received some of my best referrals to my clients' direct competitors.

3. If you have to make any prospecting cold calls (heaven forbid), they are usually much warmer to begin with. This is true for a couple of reasons. Either you've created such a reputation for yourself (or your company) that the prospect has heard of you, or because you are targeting their industry, you are able to establish credibility and value very quickly in the phone call.

Targeting a niche market is an important part of building a referral-based business because it is so much easier to create word of mouth and referrals within a niche where people interact with each other via formal and informal lines of communication. When you target a niche, you automatically provide more value, it's easier to build relationships, and you create a reputation—quite often very quickly.

C. Richard Weylman, CSP, author of *Opening Closed Doors: Keys to Reaching Hard-to-Reach People* (Irwin Professional Publishing, 1994), gives this example:

> IBM historically assigned its sales representatives to geographic areas. Its 62 geographic areas were defined clearly, and a myriad of demographic and psychographic information was available for each of these areas. However, faced with client demands that it try to do a better job of relating to and solving problems for them, IBM has redefined its markets and restructured its sales force. It now is selling to specific industries, not geographic areas or demographic profiles.
>
> No matter how you have segmented your market in the past, it is ultimately your responsibility to adjust the way you see and define the marketplace now. To demystify the process, look at how people interact and build mutually rewarding relationships with one another. You will realize quickly that they usually organize or associate with one another based on what they do for a living, or what they do for recreation. Many also organize and associate based on their social, charitable, cultural or community interests and ethnic backgrounds.

> Remember the truism: "Birds of a feather flock together." People associate and communicate with other people like themselves. For instance, people in the same type of business or profession join together in an association. To gain access to the marketplace, we should then divide it based on what our prospects do for a living, for recreation, or where they have special interests. The advantage is that by segmenting your marketing into niches in this way, you can reach out to prospects that associate and communicate with each other. This means you can find and associate with them. They, in turn, can find and associate and communicate with you. Without these two factors, your marketing and prospecting efforts will continue to be frustrating and expensive.

I have a friend who is a sales rep for an advertising agency. She says that working these principles of niche marketing is like trying to move into a new lane while waiting at a traffic light. If you begin to inch over, trying to squeeze your car into the small space between neighboring vehicles, you may not get in. However, if you just catch the eye of the driver of the car you wish to cut in front of, he or she will almost always wave you in. Establish some recognition, and you'll be let in. The same is true in your business. If people have heard of you, even if they're not sure how or where, you can get past the gatekeeper and your voice-mail messages get returned. A widespread reputation overcomes barriers.

PEOPLE BUY WHAT'S FAMILIAR

Maybe you've heard the old story of the young man who joined the military and was stationed overseas for a year. Before he left, he bought 365 postcards. He mailed one to his girlfriend every day. For about 10 months, she wrote back regularly. Then her letters stopped. When the young man returned home, he found his girlfriend married to the mailman. People buy what's familiar.

Niche marketing in a specific industry or affinity group will create that familiarity for you. Most of the referrals I have obtained over

the years have been to my clients' competitors or others within the same industry. When your clients know that you are targeting their industry and that you work from referrals, they become very willing to refer you to their colleagues. Your expertise in a niche market adds value to the relationship from the very beginning. That added value will often keep the sale from coming down to price. Earlier I mentioned that prospects who like and trust you will give you referrals. Well, when you target an industry and bring that added value—even to the very first appointment—the entire sales process is usually hastened. Your industry expertise will help you serve your prospects right from the very first meeting. Once served, they are more likely to want to introduce you to others.

FOR THE COMMITTED ONLY

Whether you are new to business and sales, or have been selling for 20 years, niche marketing will only work if you take a committed approach. Niche marketing requires a high level of commitment, not just to sales and your business, but to working the niche marketing process. This commitment will help you do what it takes to make the process work for you. If you work the process halfway, you'll get halfway results—if you're lucky. But if you're truly committed to working these strategies, then you will reach new levels of success by targeting a niche.

When you target a specific niche, your reputation becomes paramount. You need to go the extra mile. And you can't burn bridges, because word of mouth spreads faster within a niche. Every transaction, every encounter, every relationship has to be handled with the utmost of professionalism. Everyone is always a prospect, at least in the sense of helping you build your reputation. If a company is too small or doesn't really need your product or service, you still must have an attitude of service. Even people in your target industry who aren't prospects should be treated with professionalism and dignity. It takes a serious commitment to operate on this high level.

Chapter 23

Targeting Your Niche Market

"You don't want to be all things to all people."

When I started in sales, I didn't want to have anything to do with my old businesses. I wanted to start fresh. Boy, was that a mistake. My "natural market" was the network I had formed in my previous work. Once I came to my senses, I created a target market that has become tremendously successful. I know their world, so I serve them better. They know I'm targeting their industry, so they give me referrals.

Jay Morris
San Diego, CA

In this chapter, I'll give you specific tactics you can employ to make niche marketing work for you. You don't have to act on all of these ideas and techniques to make this work. In fact, you won't have the hours or the energy to undertake them all at once. However, over time, as you see these techniques yield results, read this book again to review the many things you can do to generate even more referrals and sales through focused marketing.

CHOOSE YOUR NICHE MARKET

There are three primary avenues to follow when choosing your niche market:

1. Your previous experience
2. Your existing client base
3. Your affinity to a certain niche

I did some consulting work with a company in Wisconsin that had 12 salespeople on staff. We decided that a good strategy for this business would be to have all of the salespeople target their own industry and work to create reputations for themselves and their company within each of their respective industries. We started by asking them to consider all three of the avenues stated above when choosing their target industries. If a salesperson had previous experience in an industry that demonstrated potential as a profitable niche, this was the place to start. If someone already had several clients in the same industry, this might be the place to start, or if someone just liked a certain industry, this might also be a good starting point. If they had some affinity for their target industries, the reps would enjoy establishing their reputations.

What industries have you worked for in the past? With which industries do you have some affinity? In which industry do you find fun? Answering these questions can help you narrow your focus.

Another way to find your target market is to look at your client base. With whom are you doing business now? Are there two, three,

four, or five clients in the same industry? If so, you're already niche marketing—or at least you've got a great base from which to start. You already know what their concerns are and what your solutions are. Now all you have to do is formalize your process to leverage this experience.

Are you doing work for any clients that you really enjoy? Maybe you have only one in a particular industry, but you really enjoy doing business with them—and it's profitable business. Why not focus on similar businesses?

I have a friend who decided he wanted to target an industry, so he invited several of his colleagues and other business friends over for dinner. (He happens to be a gourmet cook, but you can order take-out if you like.) He created a focus group, or what Napoleon Hill (author of *Think and Grow Rich*, Fawcett Crest, revised edition, 1960) called a *mastermind.* Hill said that when two minds come together, a third mind is created that comes up with ideas and perspectives the two minds would not achieve separately. My friend had a *mastermind* group just for himself that evening. He said, "Thank you for coming over. Let's talk about *me* for a while."

He told them what he was trying to do. He wanted to pick one, maybe two, industries within which to create a reputation over time. He asked them to help him identify the industries that were right for him. This brainstorming session gave him all sorts of ideas and strategies, and he is now successfully marketing in two industries.

DETERMINE THE UNIVERSE OF YOUR TARGET INDUSTRY

Once you have found an industry you wish to target, you must determine the universe of that industry. Is it big enough to make it worth your marketing efforts? Is it big enough within your local area, or do you have to become regional or national in your scope for the universe to be worthwhile? Are there enough prospective clients who need or want what you sell? Can they afford what you sell? Make sure there are enough qualified businesses within the niche industry as well as the geographic area where you wish to do business.

FIGURE OUT HOW TO REACH YOUR TARGET

If you cannot determine who your prospects are within a specific niche, or if they are hard to reach, this niche may not serve your purpose. Virtually every industry has a national association (some have more than one) with regional, state, and local chapters. There are various ways to acquire a list of association members. You can often find members' names on the association's website. Sometimes you are required to join the association to get access to the list. You may have a client who is a member and will loan you his or her list. If you're targeting a niche in a narrow geographic area, the phone book might be enough to do the trick.

WORK THE NUMBERS

Once you determine the universe and know that you can reach your prospects, you will want to work the numbers a little bit. You must determine sales and profit potential. If you have done business with one or more companies in your target industry, extrapolate from the volume of business you have done with them. You also want to examine the profitability of doing business in this industry, not just the total sales volume. Take a little time to run some numbers and make sure that the industry you've chosen is worth targeting.

GET TO KNOW YOUR COMPETITION

If you've picked a good industry to target, there's a strong chance someone else is already doing the same thing. Don't let that deter you. If the universe is big enough, there will be plenty of work to go around. In fact, your competitors might even welcome a fresh face with fresh ideas. Learn as much about your competitors as possible. Visit their websites. Subscribe to their e-zines. Get on their mailing lists. Obtain their promotional materials. Pick up copies of their guarantees and service policies. Watch their ads and read articles about them in the newspapers. If they are publicly traded, call your stockbroker and purchase

one share of their stock; that will put you on the mailing list for their annual report and other valuable correspondence. Call the Better Business Bureau. Learn about your competitors' strengths and weaknesses, and position yourself to be strong where they are weak.

Never talk down your competition. It's unprofessional, and it calls into question the judgment of those who have used them. If you're in front of a new prospect who has used or is using one of your competitors, saying negative things about them can destroy your credibility. Find ways to point out how you are different and better without trashing them.

On occasion I am asked how another speaker on referrals is different from me—or how my system is different from another. I usually begin my answer by saying, "If you hire Joe, you're going to get a good speaker with a great message. I believe you'll get the same from me. Here's how I think we're different and where my strengths match your situation."

FORM REFERRAL ALLIANCES WITH NICHE SUPPLIERS

Forge working relationships with other companies who serve your niche. Referrals from another salesperson or business owner can be very powerful. It's a great idea to form alliances with salespeople in non-competing companies already targeting your niche. As with all referral alliances, make sure you both know how you benefit your clients. Meet for lunch, breakfast, or over the phone every now and then to share information.

LOOK FOR OVERLAPS WITH YOUR TARGET INDUSTRY

When I started my sales training business, my first target market was the printing industry. I used to own a book publishing company, so it was a natural market for me. As I worked in the printing industry, I discovered opportunities for my company in the paper, ink, and printing equipment industries.

Today, a very large percentage of our business comes from the financial services industry. We started with insurance companies, but have since done significant work with wire houses, financial planning companies, mutual fund companies, employee benefit companies, commercial and residential real estate companies, mortgage companies, and many other related organizations.

Suppose your niche market is the hotel industry. The related industries might include resorts, food and beverage companies, cruise lines, meeting services, and entertainment companies, among others. Any major industry that you target usually has related industries that can be added to your marketing efforts. Look for these opportunities.

READ WHAT YOUR TARGET PROSPECTS ARE READING

Virtually every industry has magazines, trade journals, and newsletters (electronic and printed) that most of your niche clients and prospects read. National and local associations publish these, as do independent companies. How do you find out about them? Call the industry associations and ask what they publish. They may also be able to tell you about other publications. Talk to your existing clients or prospects within your niche and ask which industry publications they are reading. Surfing the web will probably yield great results in this endeavor.

To get a free copy of a particular publication, call the journal or magazine and ask for a current media kit. A media kit is what publications send to prospective advertisers—and I think you can legitimately call yourself a prospective advertiser. Many industry magazines and trade journals will send publications to people for free just to boost their circulation numbers so that they can charge more for their advertising. Get at least one issue of the publication, more if possible.

Read these publications to learn more about your target industry. Is this publication worth subscribing to? Is it one for which you might want to write articles? (More on this later.)

Use these publications as tools for learning about industries and identifying prospects. Remember: The more you know about prospects before you call them, the more powerful your call will be. Your local reference librarian can help you locate most of the trade journals in your target industry. You might start with *Standard Rate and Data's Business and Consumer Publications*, frequently abbreviated as SRDS. These books are usually found in the reference section of a good library. You can also find them online, but you must pay a subscription fee. Save money by using the old-fashioned way—go to your library.

Chapter 24

Cultivating Your Reputation

"It's hard to create a reputation for yourself with a shotgun approach to marketing. When you narrow your focus, a great reputation can be achieved quite easily."

In your seminar you talked about identifying "industry influencers," so I targeted every member of the board of directors in the main association in my target market. I called each one to ask for their help. I told them I was targeting their industry and really wanted to do a great job. Only 3 of the 15 agreed to meet with me, but those 3 have been so valuable. They've given me lists of industry members. They've told me what keeps their members up at night—so I know their hot buttons. And one has become a client. She's written me an incredible testimonial letter that we will turn into an endorsed mailing. Thank you!

Gretchen Slapnik
Colorado Springs, CO

Once you've determined a market to target and have learned a bit about them, it's time to start cultivating your niche. Here are proven strategies and tactics that will help you establish and leverage your reputation. I've used every one of these at one time or another.

GET INVOLVED IN INDUSTRY ASSOCIATIONS

As I mentioned in the last chapter, most industries have national, regional, state, and local associations. Oftentimes, the state and locals are affiliated with the national. One book you want to check out either in the reference section of your library or online is *The Encyclopedia of Associations*. This large book not only lists all the associations and information about them, it also indexes them in various ways, including by keywords, industries, and geographic location.

This book (and others like it) tells you how many members the associations have. (That's not the number of businesses in that industry; it's just the number of businesses that have chosen to join that particular association.) You'll discover how many conventions and other meetings they have throughout the year. Under the national association listing, they'll often detail the number of regional, state, and local associations there are. If you have difficulty finding or contacting your local association, ask the national association.

Don't rush out and join the association right away. You can usually attend a meeting as a guest before you actually have to join. I joined several associations prematurely and spent money that I didn't need to spend. Try a meeting or two as a guest. Once you are sure about your target industry, it will be time to join the association, either as a regular member or an associate member (i.e., supplier to the industry).

As a member, you will have access to products and services that can be very helpful in your target marketing efforts, such as a membership list and regular publications. After you join, be sure to get a list of all the benefits so you don't miss out on any of them.

Use the association to enhance your visibility. Richard Weylman calls it "promotion through participation." The more you become truly active, the more relationships you can forge.

Alex, a very successful financial advisor, recently headed up his target industry's annual charity event. This brought him great visibility throughout the entire year. He also worked with many centers of influence within his niche and from other parts of the business community. He told me that he can trace six new clients directly from this activity, and he feels these six clients will lead him to many others. It's just a matter of time.

IDENTIFY THE INDUSTRY INFLUENCERS

One of the most powerful things you can do to create a reputation within a target industry is identify and serve the industry influencers. You may start with the local influencers and eventually move to the national level. The industry influencers in your target industry are the presidents of the associations, members of boards, people who have had significant success within the industry, and others who are just very active in one way or another. Find ways to get to know and serve these people as soon as you can. Be sure to serve them well because they can make or break you.

Serving these people can mean making them satisfied clients, or it can mean helping them develop association projects and plan charity events. Since most of these people are very successful, they already know that the secret to success is "meeting people through other people." Once you get to know them and serve them (and not before), let them know that you're an expert in your field as it relates to their industry and that you could use their help in expanding your reputation.

When I made the decision to focus a great deal of my marketing efforts on the financial services industry, I quickly discovered that speaking at the Annual Meeting of the Million Dollar Round Table would be a great move for me. I gained the opportunity to speak at the MDRT by first identifying the industry influencers on my local level. I learned who was involved in the committees who chose the event's speakers. I provided them with my promotional materials, and several heard me speak at local meetings. In other words, I used *referrals* to become known and was eventually nominated to speak at the annual meeting. I've spoken to this prestigious group twice, creating a reputation among its members that has been quite a plus for my business.

WRITE ARTICLES FOR INDUSTRY PUBLICATIONS

Write articles that relate to your product or service as it is used by your target industry. A printing salesperson could write an article on how to find the right printer or how to better understand the new digital technology. Someone who sells financial services could write articles that teach people about the latest investment options. Write articles that teach your target industry how to better utilize your type of product or service. Practical knowledge is the key. Checklists, quizzes, and the like are always popular.

This article cannot be one long advertisement for you and your company. It should be full of useful information. The purpose here is not to sell; it is to establish yourself as an expert. Trade journals usually won't run a piece that's too self-promotional, and even if they do, readers will not appreciate it.

Many good things can happen when you have articles published in industry publications. You can make reprints of the article, adding the banner from the front of the publication. When you send out information to prospects, you can use the reprint to demonstrate that you specialize in their industry. Send the reprints to current clients in your target industry as another way of staying in touch. Use the reprints to follow up with prospects in your pipeline.

Exposure in industry journals and magazines is a great way to get you past the gatekeeper or through the voice-mail barrier of new prospects because your reputation precedes you.

PRODUCE A COMPANY NEWSLETTER

If you don't already put out a regular newsletter, it may be time for you to get serious about this great communication device. These days,

most companies are publishing electronic newsletters delivered via e-mail. At this writing, our newsletter—*The Referral Minute*—currently has more than 19,000 subscribers. This electronic newsletter for financial professionals is delivered twice per month, with occasional special editions throughout the year. We have recently started a second e-mail newsletter for a more general business audience. If you'd like to subscribe to either newsletter, visit our website at www.ReferrralCoach.com. Not only will you receive a continual flow of useful information about referrals, you'll observe how we use our newsletter to deliver value, build our reputation, and generate business. You can model what we do for your own newsletter.

Of course, the most effective newsletter you could produce would be exclusively for your target industry. If you decide to put out a generic newsletter, make sure that all of its contents are in some way relevant to your target industry.

WRITE SPECIAL REPORTS, BOOKLETS, AND E-BOOKS

Now that we have moved from the Industrial Age to the Information Age, there is no better way to create a reputation as an expert in your target industry than to provide information to your prospects and clients. To this end, many people who target industries create small information booklets or "special reports." A 16 to 32-page publication can relate your product or service to your prospects' and clients' industry and buying situation. While this publication has information about your product/service, it is not a *promotional* piece. It is an *educational* piece. As you educate your prospects and clients, they recognize you as the expert. They want to do business with you and they will give you referrals.

In most cases you should give this report away for free, but always put a price on it to increase the perceived value. A general report might be titled "How to Buy Printing," "How to Buy Your Next Computer," "How to Select a Real Estate Agent to Help You Sell Your Home," "How to Select a Financial Planner," or "How to Buy Hotel

Meeting Services." A more specific, timely report might be called "How the New Round of Tax Laws Affects Your Investment Strategy" or "How to Purchase Printing in This Digital World." You get the idea.

This report can be a great icebreaker for new contacts, a follow-up item to keep the selling courtship alive, a thank you for new clients, or a way to stay in touch with existing clients. It will be most powerful if it is targeted to one specific industry and says so on the cover. (For example, "What Hotels Should Look For in Their Next Computer Upgrade.") A generic publication can still be effective, but it must be written in such a way that it is completely relevant to your target industry.

While e-books (books delivered electronically) have become quite popular, I believe that a printed and bound book or report has more perceived value. You should consider doing both. At ReferralCoach.com, many of our publications are available as printed works as well as e-books.

USE MEDIA PUBLICITY

Did you know that anywhere from 50 to 80 percent of the stories in your newspaper were placed there through press releases and other publicity efforts? It's true. Beyond the front page news, most of the stories that appear in newspapers and magazines are there because someone is pushing that topic, issue, or newsworthy event to the press. Someone persuades an editor that the information is of interest to readers, and as a result, an article is born.

The key to getting an article placed or an event covered is to make sure that it's newsworthy. It must contain information that will benefit readers. Taking a strong, even controversial, stand on an issue will get media and reader attention. If what you have to say is powerful and helpful, you stand a chance of being published. As soon as I finish writing this book, I will write a series of articles designed to help me publicize it. My first article is entitled "It's Time to Put Cold Calling on Ice." I will talk about how cold calling is a dying sales strategy. This is somewhat controversial because some people are still having some

success with cold calling, but that success will diminish quickly as people get harder to reach by phone and the do-not-call lists grow in size.

Rarely does a large newspaper or magazine print a press release word for word, but smaller publications quite often do. I've had many press releases printed exactly as I had written them. People say, "Bill, that was a great article I saw about you in such-and-such publication." In response, I say, "Yeah, it was, thanks." And I wrote it. It was my press release!

Create releases that are newsworthy. Let's say you sell employee benefits, and your niche is the hotel industry. Making a large sale to a well-known company is a newsworthy event. Just make sure you get permission from your new client to publicize the sale. Every time your company comes out with a new product or service that will benefit your target industry, write a press release designed to make it look as if the product or service was created just for that industry.

Remember the fundamental selling principle: Talk about your features in terms of benefits. When you mention a new product, new location, or any other feature of your company worth writing about in a press release, always put it in terms of its benefits to your clients. "XYZ Company Has Moved to a New Location to Better Serve Clients."

All you need to do is contact the magazine, journal, or newsletter and ask who should receive a press release on the topic you plan to cover. Then send it on. If you have a publicity photo (which you should), send that as well. Many small publications give preference to press releases and articles submitted with photos.

There are many books available that teach the fine points of writing press releases. Consult one and follow its guidelines before sending yours off. If you try to wing it, your odds of having your press release considered will decrease.

The important thing about approaching the press with news releases or a story idea is that it cannot appear to be self-serving. Certainly you can be quoted in the release or article, and your product or service should be mentioned, but don't let read like one long ad. It must be newsworthy.

If your press release prompts the publication to write a full article on your subject, a reporter may call some of your competitors to gain other perspectives. That's fine. Your product or service will only look better by comparison.

With this new awareness, look at some of the articles in newspapers, magazines, and especially trade journals. Look at the headlines and the topics being discussed. What similar topics can you write about that relate to your product or service? You're not a good writer? That's all right. Just talk your thoughts into a tape recorder, transcribe them, and then find an editor. Ask a friend, a loved one, or a professional to edit your news release at a reasonable rate.

CREATE EDUCATIONAL OPPORTUNITIES

Many companies invite prospects and clients into their offices or plants to show them the latest updates in their industry. Some companies sponsor these events in hotels. Use your imagination to come up with educational opportunities for your target industry. Even if you are not in the training business, can you go in-house and conduct some training programs, maybe teach them how to use your product or service better? Host a luncheon. Sponsor other speakers. These events cannot be ads for you and your company. You really must deliver useful information.

Educational events will serve at least two purposes: First, they will establish you and your company as the experts in your field, especially as it relates to your target industry. Second, these events give you another warm way to meet with prospects and clients. Invite your current clients to bring their industry colleagues to these events. This way you can be introduced in person to a new prospect by a satisfied client.

SPONSOR AN EVENT

Your target industry is probably full of opportunities for you to gain widespread recognition through sponsorship. Perhaps your target industry has awards ceremonies, and the awards are sponsored in

some way. Perhaps your target industry, particularly on a local level, sponsors certain charities. Determine the various industry events and find ways to attach your name to those events through sponsorship. Make the sponsorship directly from you, not just your company. Instead of the brochure saying, "This award is being sponsored by XYZ Company," have it say, "This award is being sponsored by John Doe of XYZ Company."

MASTER PUBLIC SPEAKING

When you target a specific industry or affinity group, speaking in front of groups within your niche can be a powerful way to attract new clients. Your speech demonstrates your expertise.

ADAPT YOUR MARKETING MATERIALS

A brochure or other promotional piece will always be more effective if it's tailored to your niche. With a tailored brochure, your prospects and clients will see your value to them. To which company and salesperson would you give extra consideration—one with a generic product/service or one with an offering that's tailored to your industry? Your materials should be designed to attract your ideal clients.

PLACE ADS YOUR PROSPECTS WILL SEE

Remember: People buy what's familiar. Given the choice between some person or product they've heard of before and one that's unknown to them, they'll usually go with what's familiar. If you don't believe this, the next time you're in the grocery store, watch yourself make buying decisions. We all buy what's familiar, not necessarily because we think it's a better product, but to minimize the risk of making a bad decision. That's why advertising works.

Advertising *does* work, depending on what you want it to do. Once you have progressed in your target marketing activities, perhaps

6 months to a year down the road, consider investing in some well-placed advertising. I say "consider" because I've seen so many businesses waste money on advertising. Advertising generally does not bring in sales unless you have a very specific offer. Advertising creates an impression. Sometimes those impressions are very valuable if you are trying to present yourself as an expert in an industry. Your ads in industry publications create familiarity.

For instance, your local industry association may publish a newsletter that includes people's business card ads or similar small ads. This might be of value to you. It is an economical way to create familiarity. When you reach prospects on the phone, they will have heard of you, and they will associate you with their industry.

Here is an important thing to keep in mind when considering advertising: Don't be your own copywriter. It's not your expertise. Hire a pro. Otherwise you may be throwing good money down the drain.

CREATE A REPUTATION WITH DIRECT MAIL

Staying with the theme "People buy what's familiar," consider using direct mail to target your industry. Again, I use the word "consider" because I have seen so many businesses waste so much money on direct mail. They think these beautiful mailing pieces are going to bring in business, and they just don't. They do create positive impressions for the people who open the mail, but as you know too well, they don't always get opened. Direct mail can have a place as part of your familiarity mix. In fact, it can play a powerful role. The key is repetition. If you have the choice of mailing to 6000 people once or 2000 people three times, go with the latter. The more they see from you, the more they are likely to actually read what you send.

When you decide to implement a direct-mail strategy, budget for at least three pieces to each person on your list. Better yet, make the program ongoing—anywhere from 4 to 12 mailings per year. Consider using post cards. They're less expensive to print and mail, and the recipient doesn't have to open anything to get your message.

There are many books on how to use direct mail effectively. I recommend that you seek this advice. If you want to create a reputation in a target industry, begin a simple mailing program—and keep it simple. If it isn't, you probably won't keep it going. If you don't keep it going, you'll just be *spending* your money, not *investing* it!

HARNESS THE POWER OF TESTIMONIAL LETTERS

Even if you aren't yet targeting a niche market, you should be collecting testimonial letters. These third-party endorsements can be enormously helpful in establishing your credibility and value. These letters become part of your information packet, and they can provide evidence to your prospects that you've targeted their industry. Refer to Appendix B for details on the most effective ways to collect testimonials.

MODIFY EXISTING PRODUCTS AND SERVICES, OR CREATE NEW ONES

As you begin to learn the needs of your target industry, you can look for ways to modify products and services or even create new ones that are tailored specifically to your target industry. The more you learn about your target industry, the more creative you can be with products and services for it.

Chapter 25

Your Target Marketing Plan

"Failing to plan is like planning to fail."

Everyone in my office uses a shotgun approach to their business. When I finally committed to a target market, my sales doubled. I have now led my company in sales for the last 6 months.

BILL MILLER
WICHITA, KS

WHO DO YOU KNOW WHO PRACTICES TARGET MARKETING?

Now that you know what target marketing is all about, stop and think: Do you know any salespeople or small business owners who are targeting specific industries? If you do, I suggest you make an appointment to have breakfast or lunch with them—to learn from them.

If you want target marketing to work for you, you must create a plan and then work the plan. (A trite phrase, yes, but oh so true!) First, identify the ideas in this book that you are likely to do right away. This becomes your short-term plan. Then identify the things that you'll do down the road when you have a little more time or you've enjoyed a little success. This becomes part of your mid-range plan. Create a time line and put reminders in your calendar to keep things moving.

It should go without saying (but I'll say it anyway) that this plan must be flexible. As you learn more about what you're doing, you'll need to change and adapt. I heard an expression that fits perfectly: "Well begun is half done." When you begin with a sturdy plan that allows flexibility, you are halfway to your goal.

Another key element in making niche marketing work for you, especially if you work for someone else, is to gain support from others (such as your boss). That's why it's important to run the numbers. Attractive gross and net potentials will help you establish buy-in from others. This support from above is important because you will be engaged in some activities that will not yield instant results. Researching prospects at the library, developing direct-mail pieces and other ways to communicate with your target industry, creating brochures, writing journal articles, and attending association meetings will all lead to increased business, but not immediately. Your supervisor must buy in to your goals and methods, or he or she will be hard to sustain.

DEVELOP YOUR MARKET PROFILE

It's very important that you create a market profile of the industry that you are targeting. This will help you determine the quality of your target market.

I will take you step by step through a market profile. (This was inspired by Jim Cathcart.) First, take out a clean piece of paper and write, "Market Profile" at the top. Then answer the following questions as best you can. This process may take a few sittings.

1. *The market*: What is the name of the industry or affinity group that you are planning to target?
2. *The demographics*: How many potential prospects are there? How many of these companies are there locally, regionally, nationally, and even internationally? Call the associations; they'll tell you. Find out how many of these companies are the right size for you to do business with. For instance, there are about 75,000 printers in the United States, but probably less than a third of them have a sales staff large enough to make it worthwhile for me to prospect them. That's still a big audience to target.
3. *Organizations to which they belong*: What national, regional, state, and local associations are involved with this industry? Often there are two or three national associations, and most have local chapters. *The Encyclopedia of Associations* in your library will tell you what you need to know, and the national associations can give you a list of the smaller chapters.
4. *Publications they read*: What publications do they read? Find out by calling the industry associations and by calling the people you already know in the industry.
5. *Meetings they attend*: What meetings, conventions, conferences, and trade shows are part of your target market? Again, you can find this out easily from the associations and people you already know in the industry.
6. *Industry influencers*: Who are the industry influencers? Find this out from associations and people in the industry. Sometimes you can discover the names you need right away, and other times it takes longer. Begin with a local scope, and then go national when it's appropriate for you. Usually members of the association's board of directors and past presidents

are industry influencers. Which are the largest, most successful, most respected businesses? Who is being featured in the industry publications? Every time you meet people in your target industry, ask them who the industry influencers are (besides them, of course). You can also try searching the Internet using specific terms and names to see who comes up most frequently.

7. *Needs, fears, and goals*: What are their common needs, fears, and goals? What are the issues of the people within the industry you're targeting? List these on your market profile. As you learn more, add them to your list. These needs, fears, and goals are the stuff of your positioning strategy. Learn how to speak about the benefits of your product or service in terms of their concerns and goals.

A market profile is critical to giving you a good handle on how best to serve this target industry. Make one now and revise it every 6 months or even more often.

There you have it: Niche marketing, the fourth competency in building a referral business. This is the most powerful way to create a situation in which you establish a reputation as an expert, as it relates to your product or service, and leave those cold calls behind you. You can leverage that expertise and reputation so that people call you, and when you call prospects, they know who you are and want to talk to you.

Work these strategies and your sales will increase significantly over the next couple of years—and you'll enjoy the selling process so much more!

Chapter 26

Putting It All Together

"I don't know what your destiny will be, but one thing I know, the only ones among you who will be really happy are those who have sought and found how to serve."

ALBERT SCHWEITZER

I wanted to tell you what my new referral mindset has done for me. First, I'm paying closer attention to my customer service. I know now that I'm not just trying to make a sale or keep a customer. I'm also trying to get that customer to tell others about me. And second, I've realized that if I'm going to build a referral-based business, I have to make it happen, I can't just sit around and wait for it to happen. I'm asking for referrals, planting seeds, and networking like crazy. I'm even looking for a niche to focus most of my marketing efforts on. Since I've been using your concepts, I've increased sales by 250 percent in 2 years. Incredible!

STEVEN SELLERS
MINNEAPOLIS, MN

THE WAY OF THE WORLD

One of my business slogans is, "The way of the world is meeting people through other people, and the referral is the warm way we get into their lives." I hope I've demonstrated to you the enormous advantage you can create for yourself when you form great relationships with prospects and clients, serve people well (be they clients, prospects, or referral alliances), and constantly think in terms of how you can leverage those relationships to create more win/win situations (that go beyond the buyer/seller relationship).

To generate an unlimited and predictable supply of high-quality referrals, you must expand your thinking. Every business relationship you enter into has the potential to lead you to other relationships. Marketing expert Dr. Thomas Stanley calls this "offering more than the core." You find ways to move your relationships with clients to a level of mutual assistance that goes beyond the core product or service that brought you together in the first place.

PEOPLE WILL SPREAD THE WORD ABOUT YOU

When you serve people, they naturally want to help you back, as well as bring your good value to others. Many people love to have a stake in the success of other people—people like you whom they like and trust.

Not long ago, I was teaching my referral strategies to a group of salespeople. The sessions went well, and most of the salespeople started getting more referrals immediately. Of course, those referrals translated into an increase in sales. However, one salesperson, Bruce, was struggling with this referral stuff. He called me and asked if we could meet for breakfast before the next sales meeting. When we got together, Bruce told me that he wanted to use referrals more but some block was stopping him. With a little exploration, this is what I helped him figure out.

Bruce wanted to be successful by his own efforts—he wanted to "do it himself." Just between you and me, I think he was trying to

prove to his father (who was quite successful and had a very strong personality) that he could do it on his own. For some reason, Bruce felt that asking for referrals—asking for help—was not doing it on his own, so he found it difficult to ask for referrals. I helped Bruce reframe his thinking. I asked him, "Do you serve your clients well so they keep coming back?"

"Yes."

"Do your clients like you and trust you?"

"Yes."

"The times you've gotten referrals without asking, did you convert them into sales and create more happy clients who like you and trust you?"

"Yes."

Then I said, "Who do you think is doing that? You're doing that! You are serving your clients so well, you are creating such good relationships with them that if you only asked, they would be thrilled to help you and bring your value to others. You created that. You deserve to be rewarded even more than you are now. Many of these people want to give back to you and give your value to others. You just have to get it started."

I'm happy to say that Bruce "got it." He stepped out of his comfort zone a few times to ask for referrals. To his amazement, they came easily. He converted most of those referrals into new clients. For Bruce, the chain reaction has begun. He is now on his way to creating an unlimited supply of referrals because he now realizes that referrals from his clients are the highest form of praise he can receive. Now it's in his constant awareness to create relationships and serve clients so well that they want to give him referrals!

WORKING FROM REFERRALS IS A MINDSET

To create a steady flow of referrals, you must develop a referral mindset. Not a day should go by where you're not working on becoming more referable, planting seeds, asking for referrals, and sending thank you gifts for referrals. Referral marketing must be "top of mind awareness."

You must constantly say to yourself, "I sell a quality product or service. I deliver incredible service. People like me and trust me. I deserve to get referrals. I serve people so well that they want to refer people to me. I deserve this highest form of praise."

THE ATTITUDE OF SERVICE

Do you have a true attitude of service? Are you constantly looking for ways to serve others?

Are you serving your prospects long before you sell them anything? Do you think "process" instead of "products?" Do you ask questions that get people thinking in new ways? Do you help them think "big picture"? Are you giving referrals to your clients as well as to other salespeople? Are you getting to know your clients in such a manner that you can bring value to their lives in ways that go far beyond what you sell? If you are doing these things, then you have an attitude of service, and you will have very little difficulty generating referrals—as long as you remember to ask for them.

If you don't have an attitude of service, your ability to gain referrals will be severely limited. Zig Ziglar says it this way: "You can get everything in life you want, if you just help enough other people get what they want."

THE POWER OF LEVERAGE

"Master the power of leverage . . . to build real business with long-term strength." So says Bill Brooks, author, speaker, and sales expert. Just as you must have an attitude of service to create a steady and predictable flow of referrals, it helps to have an attitude of leverage.

I look at it this way: For many years, the prospecting process was likened to a pipeline. You fill one end of the pipeline with qualified prospects. As you put them through your sales process, a few

new clients drip out of the other end. In this model, the salesperson's job is to keep the funnel full. This is activity-based prospecting. While it's a model that can produce results, it takes a great deal of time, energy, money, and sweat to produce results. One problem with this model is that oftentimes people begin to confuse activity with accomplishment.

While having enough activity is always important, you want to shift your thinking from an activity-based prospecting process to a relationship-based process. Instead of just thinking, "How can I keep my pipeline full?" or "How can I make this sale?" you begin to ask yourself, "How can I make this sale, and how can this relationship lead me to other business?" If you aspire to build a base of satisfied clients and referral alliances, you can constantly tap into this base for more business. This is leverage!

Legendary sales trainer Larry Wilson says, "Be careful of spending time with business that has no leveragability. No business should pass through you without putting it to the leveragability test." From my perspective, this doesn't mean you don't take non-leveragable business. It does means that you are always looking for this leverage angle right from the beginning of each relationship. If you have this awareness, or attitude of leverage, you're more likely to see the opportunities.

Please understand that the leverage I'm talking about is not manipulation or going for lopsided wins. Leveraging relationships should always be a two-way, win/win proposition.

A SOLID FOUNDATION AND COMPETENCIES

Before I send you out into the real world to take action on these ideas, I'd like to remind you of the essence of each part of this book. With that, I'll leave the rest up to you.

First, we laid the foundation by talking about two fundamentals in selling: relationships and service. The quality of the relationships you form is what allows everything else to be possible. Your attitude of service helps you build a trusting relationship in which each party can keep winning for years to come.

Then we covered the four competencies of building your referral business. The first competency is "Enhance your referability through service." There are three main thoughts I want to leave you with:

1. To exceed your clients' expectations, you must understand their expectations. You must discover why you got their business, how the other guy lost their business, what it will take to make them happy, and what it will take to keep them happy. With this knowledge, you can make them say "Wow!" every time you serve them.
2. Don't run away from the problems. When a problem arises, don't even flinch. Just be there and start working for a solution as best you can. Make it easy for clients to complain; in fact, encourage it. Remember: A relationship that's had a problem that's been handled well is a stronger relationship than one that's never had a problem. You can brag about your problem-free relationships, but if I were you, I'd brag about the relationships in which you fixed the problems.
3. Help clients reduce their stress. Make dealing with you an oasis in their busy lives. Anticipate their needs, discover their stresses, and serve them beyond their expectations.

The second competency is "Prospect for referrals." Take control of your destiny (as much as any mortal can) and be proactive in gaining referrals. When you ask for referrals, do so in a way that lets your sources know that it's important, not just to you, but to the people they can help you serve. Ask for their help in helping others. Upgrade the quality of your referrals as much as possible. Consider getting introduced to your new prospects instead of calling them out of the blue. Always keep your referral sources informed of the progress of the referral, and always thank them for their referrals.

The third competency is "Strategic networking." Identify and meet the right people (and businesses) in your world that have the

ability to refer business to you, even though they may never become clients themselves. Make sure these folks know what you do and how you truly benefit others. Make sure you know what they do and how they truly benefit others. Then find ways to continually serve each other. Network with the best networkers.

Sales expert Steven Sullivan sums it up well: "As I reflected back on all the great salesmen I've known, a common thread ran through the fabric of their individual selling style. No, it is not creativity, intelligence, sense of urgency, or communication skills. What they share with each other is an ability to build a successful network, a group of individuals whom they motivate to support and sustain their efforts. They recognize they are not an island unto themselves. They realize no matter how great their individual talent, it pales in comparison to a supporting cast." Richard Weylman says, "Successful people are interdependent, not independent."

Finally, the fourth competency is "Target niche markets." When you create a reputation in a target industry, the referrals will flow effortlessly. Having expertise in a target industry will allow you to bring value to the table that none of your competitors can. Pick an industry you like and establish a reputation for yourself. You'll have more fun, and you'll be more successful.

Work on any one of these competencies and referrals will come your way. Work a little on all four and even more referrals will come your way. Master all four competencies and you'll create a steady and predictable flow of high-quality clients through referrals. You'll be living a referral lifestyle. Your business will boom, even in a slow economy.

Appendix A

The Importance of Process

Selling a product or a service does not make you referable. It's the *process* of doing business with you (and your company) that makes you referable. It's much harder to generate referrals in a transactional business than it is with a process-oriented business.

To build a referral-based business, you must think *process* over *products*.

A NEW ECONOMY?

In their book *The Experience Economy* (Harvard Business School Press), Joseph Pine and James Gilmore examine what it takes to create word of mouth and getting your clients to tell others about you. To make their point, they use the metaphor of coffee beans. It goes something like this:

If I were to travel to South America and buy a pound of freshly picked coffee beans, it would cost me about 25 cents a pound. Coffee beans are a *commodity*. If I went into a grocery store here in the States, a pound of coffee grounds would cost me about $4.50 depending on the brand and part of the country I was in. Coffee grounds are *goods*.

If I purchased a cup of coffee in a diner, I would be paying about $12 to $15 per pound of beans. Brewing coffee is a *service*. Then there's Starbucks. Starbucks is an *experience*.

The original premise behind Starbucks was to re-create the Italian coffee experience. I think everyone will agree that Starbucks has been wildly successful. Commodities are interchangeable. Goods are tangible. Services are intangible. Most financial professionals play on the level of goods and services. You talk about the products you sell and you talk about the service you provide. There's nothing wrong with that. Those are important topics. However, you're missing opportunities to create word of mouth if you don't think in terms of creating great experiences. Experiences are *memorable*. Memorable experiences create word of mouth.

AND YOUR PROCESS IS...?

Do you have a clearly defined process through which you put most of your new clients? Do you help think "big picture"? Do you educate them? Do you help them set specific goals? Do you question their assumptions? Do you lead them to make the right decisions and stop procrastinating? Do you use the same process virtually every time, or do you wing it?

Take a minute to think about the process through which you put your prospects and clients from the minute you first contact them all the way to when they become clients and beyond. Are you creating "memorable experiences"?

LEVERAGING YOUR PROCESS

Here are five steps that will ensure you get the most out of your process to make your clients happy and generate word of mouth:

1. Have a clearly defined process that is repeatable and be clear about how your clients benefit.

2. Name your process. When you name your process, it becomes yours. No one else has your process. Clients can get this process only from you. This is a way to distinguish yourself in this crowded marketplace.
3. Illustrate your process with graphic illustrations. This brings your process to life. It helps you explain your process to your clients and centers of influence.
4. Communicate to prospects, clients, and centers of influence why and how your process is beneficial. Get in the habit of talking about your process on a regular basis.
5. Bring your process to life with stories, anecdotes, and case studies.

Your mantra from now on—if you want to become referable quickly in your relationships and remain referable throughout—is "process, not products." A good process will lead to many product sales repeatedly throughout your relationships.

For Instance

Here's an example: If a financial professional sells you a life insurance policy, it's not the selling of the policy that makes that financial professional referable. It's the process she puts you through to determine how much life insurance you need and what type of insurance is best for you. To do that, she must first know what's important to you: about money, about how you want to take care of your family once you're gone, about how much federal tax you want to protect your estate from, and so on. To do the best job for you, she must first assist you with some big-picture thinking. She must educate you about the decision you're making. She might even have to question some of your assumptions and get you to think in ways you haven't thought in before. Through this process, she becomes referable, not through the sale of a specific product.

Appendix B

Collect and Use Testimonial Letters

Testimonial letters are a close cousin to referrals. Like referrals, they are a part of the "body of evidence" you need to help a prospect feel good about becoming your client.

COLLECTING THE LETTERS

If I know my client is particularly pleased, I always ask for a letter. I'll say, "I really appreciate your saying that. You know, every now and then it's helpful for me to get a letter from a satisfied client. Would you be willing to take a couple of minutes to put what you just said to me in writing and send it to me on your letterhead?" I don't think I've ever had anyone refuse to write a letter for me.

However, getting them to follow through on that agreement is another issue.

I've found that if I just leave it at that simple request, I get about 40 percent of the letters promised. People don't mean to break their word; they're just busy, like everyone else. That's why I usually keep the process going. As soon as I hang up the phone, I send them an e-mail thanking them for their kind words and thanking them "in advance" for the letter they'll be sending. This is a subtle reminder in the form of a thank you.

If my happy client is an industry influencer or a center of influence, I definitely want a letter from her. If I haven't received the letter within a month or so, I'll call her on the phone. The client usually brings up the letter first and apologizes for not getting to it yet. Then I say, "That's okay, I know you're really busy. Here's an idea: Would it be helpful if I put a few thoughts on paper for you? You can edit or rewrite all you like and then send it to me on your letterhead, okay?" People always agree to this.

First, I make sure I take some notes on what they found valuable about the work I do so I can use some of their own words. Then I send it to them via e-mail. It's quite simple. I've collected dozens of letters this way. You may feel this is a very gutsy question to ask, and perhaps it is, but I've never had anyone refuse. In fact, they're usually relieved at my offer.

I used to suggest when I first requested the letter that I write it, however, I've found that the letters clients write themselves are usually better than mine. Therefore, I resort to helping them only when it's a letter I really want and they are dragging their feet.

USING THE TESTIMONIALS

Mark works for a customized manufacturing company in Philadelphia. The day after attending one of my seminars, he put these testimonial techniques to work when he got a call from a very happy client. Not only was she pleased with Mark's service, but she was also impressed with how the production staff had handled some problems that came up with her job. Mark asked her to write a letter—and specifically requested that she mention the production staff in it.

When the letter arrived, Mark shared it with the people who had produced this job. The production folks were pleased to know that the client appreciated their hard work. They were pleased with Mark for showing them the letter. Do you think this will help Mark when he

needs more favors from production? You bet it will. Do you think the production staff will take care of this client the next time? Count on it.

When you collect testimonial letters, it's a good idea to get a few that speak about the other people who help you deliver great service. These letters will help you with both your internal relationships and your prospecting. As your prospects look through your letters, they will see people saying good things about you, and one or two saying good things about your team.

Use these letters liberally. Put them in your information packets. Use them to follow up with prospects you're still courting. Use short excerpts from them in brochures and newsletters. Often, when I send out a testimonial letter, I highlight a sentence or paragraph I really want my prospect to read. I increase the chances of getting the letter read by calling attention to it. Usually, in the PS of my cover letter I'll say something like, "Check out what other satisfied clients have said about our work." This also increases the chances of them reading the letters.

I've consulted with several companies that take this a step further. They create special printed pieces with a photo of the happy client's face or place of business next to his or her testimonial letter. This strengthens the impact of the testimony, and the clients enjoy the recognition.

Use third-party endorsements. They work!

It is important that you make a habit of collecting testimonial letters. Use them every time you give or mail promotional literature to prospects. Sometimes I just send a couple of testimonial letters instead of my fancy brochure and the whole promotional kit. (I keep track of everything I send to my prospects and clients, including which testimonial letters have gone to whom.)

Buy reams of different rag-content paper in various business colors (nothing too bright). Then copy the testimonial letters onto this higher-quality paper. These letters will certainly stand out and get read more than letters on plain white paper. I've just started doing this myself, and it makes my promotional kit look much more polished.

Index

About the Author

Bill Cates is the president of Referral Coach International and is considered the nation's foremost expert on how to increase sales through high-quality referrals and word-of-mouth. Bill works with salespeople who want to master the referral process and with companies who want to build a stronger referral culture.

Bill's Unlimited Referrals Marketing System® has been featured in such publications as *Success Magazine*, *Entrepreneur* magazine, and *Selling Power* magazine. Plus, his own business success has been featured in *Money* magazine.

Bill writes columns for *On Wall Street* magazine and *Advisor Today*. Bill's clients include such companies as American Express Financial Advisors, Andersen Windows, Merrill Lynch, Mutual of Omaha, Mass-Mutual Financial Group, Bankers Life, State Farm, and many others.